The Pen that Set Mexico on Fire:

The Betrayal of Ricardo Flores Magón During the Revolution

By

Steve Devitt

First published in the United States of America in 2017 by Henselstone Verlag LLC

First Edition

Every effort has been made to locate and contact all holders of copyright to material reproduced in this book.

For information about permission to reproduce selections from this book, write to Henselstone Verlag LLC, P.O. Box 201, Amissville, VA 20106.

Library of Congress Control Number 2017932044

Keyword Data

Devitt, Stephen, 1947-

The Pen that set Mexico on Fire: The Betrayal of Ricardo Flores Magón during the Revolution / Stephen Devitt.

p. cm

Includes biographical references and index.

ISBN 978-0-9969554-5-4

1.   United States – History – World War I – 1914 to 1917
2.   Mexico – History – Porfiriato – 1900 to 1911
3.   Mexico – History – Revolution, 1910-1920 – Diplomatic History
4.   United States – Foreign Relations – Mexico
5.   Mexico – Foreign Relations – United States
6.   Mexico – Politics – Anarchism
7.   Mexico – Journalism
8.   Mexico – Newspaper Publishing
I.   Devitt, Stephen. Title.

Printed in the of America United States

Chinua Achebe said that those who would canonize [the] past must serve as the devil's advocate setting down beside the glories every inconvenient fact. Our world is going through a difficult relationship with facts and at a time when the role of journalists is being challenged by despots (new and old) and those who wish to obfuscate truth, this book serves as cautionary set of facts.

Elnathan John
satirist | novelist

The Pen that set Mexico on Fire is filled with printed voices called out of the past. Nor are they subjugated in service of authorial intent; they speak for themselves, echoing out of the narrative as the scenes change. Giving RFM his proper due feels like a matter of respect and honor when one reads Devitt's book, a tip of the hat from one newspaperman and writer to another.

Dr. Alexander Chirila
writer | university professor | mystic | and traveler

A man in prison, his intellectual power diminishing in the years of solitary confinement and medical neglect. Outside, thousands of miles away, the Mexican Revolution ravages communities of Indios, laborers, workers, and anyone in the path of the destructive rage of revolutionary fervor. Ricardo Flores Magón planted the seeds of destruction and upheaval as a journalist and activist for the forgotten masses of Mexico. In the end, the forces of old and new, many of which he had set free, destroyed him. What remains are ideas and the work of a brilliant newspaper man.

Heribert von Feilitzsch
historian | author

Steve Devitt started writing for publication in 1963. As a junior in high school he wrote for his school paper in Billings Montana. He worked his way through college on journalism scholarships. He became the youngest editor in Montana in 1969, working at the *Choteau Acantha*, a hot-lead weekly. Before moving on to teach university level English and writing classes in 1994, he edited a half dozen weeklies, two daily newspapers and had a successful career as a freelance writer. Since then, he has taught in the United States, China and Nigeria.

In the 1970s, he wrote for what was then called "the underground press." He was an associate editor of the College Press Service, served as news editor of the Vancouver, BC, *Georgia Strait*. In 1980, he founded the *Montana Maverick*, a weekly he published for three years.

He lives in Tucson, Ariz., with his wife Suyun, and Mr. Dog.

Table of Contents

List of Illustrations

Editor's Note

Over the past two years Steve Devitt and I have exchanged over 1,000 e-mails, almost all of them discussing history in general and the Mexican Revolution in particular. An accomplished investigative journalist and small town newspaper man, Devitt (as his friends call him) has brought a totally fresh perspective of the Mexican Revolution to me. Irreverently, he dismisses the pompous historians on the topic who claim truth as a matter of authority. This irreverence had attracted him to my work, and he has made me an admirer of his. The first manuscript I read was his thesis on the Mexican press during the *Porfiriato*. It is a master piece.

Devitt's research started in the years of writing this thesis, when he interviewed first hand witnesses of the Revolution such as Margarita Terrazas and leading journalists of Mexico such as Mario Beauregard, Gabriel Molina and others. The central question of Devitt's research quickly arises, namely why the Díaz regime fought Mexican independent journalists with such fervor. Devitt reveals the answer in his picture of Ricardo Flores Magón, an excellent journalist and newspaperman. Together with other journalistic heroes such as Daniel Cabrera and Filomena Mata, he published ten years before the violent upheaval of the Revolution what were the devastating truths of a corrupt and repressive regime. These early revolutionaries had no weapons other than their pens, archaic printing equipment and rudimentary means of distribution that both the US authorities and the Díaz regime did their very best to suppress. They could not stop a determined, driven and idealistic personality like Ricardo Flores Magón.

From his chosen exile, Ricardo Flores Magón sent 30,000 copies of *Regeneración* along the railroads from the southern border of the United States into every village in Mexico on a weekly basis to be read by the local school teacher, the few residents who could read, and dissatisfied Mexican elites. Magón's readers included Francisco and Gustavo Madero, Emiliano Zapata, Pascual Orozco, Abraham Gonzalez, Álvaro Obregón, Venustiano Carranza, and scores of future revolutionary leaders and followers. That is the important fact about the influence of the Magóns on the Revolution. It is not, as historians want to make us believe, that after the Revolution broke out in 1910, Magón's political views had shifted so far to the left that he alienated the very same people whose revolutionary fire he had stoked in the years leading up to the violent upheaval.

Ricardo Flores Magón had predicted and encouraged violent social struggle in Mexico. He was one of the few who knew that merely changing the faces of Mexican leadership would not settle the deep grievances in a country of dispossessed Indian communities, landless peons, exploited workers, and a new middle class without political clout. Magón predicted social revolution based on the facts he as a journalist knew to be true.

Devitt's fresh view of the Mexican Revolution through the eyes of the fourth pillar of Democracy reminds all of us that the first sign of repression is the elimination of the free press. As someone, whose grandfather was a journalist who spent large parts of the Hitler regime in concentration camps because he dared to publish the truth, I am proud and privileged to have had a hand in publishing this important new insight into the origins of the Mexican Revolution.

Heribert von Feilitzsch

Acknowledgements

(Don't skip this. The story starts here)

Τhis book would not have been written had it not been for Heribert von Feilitzsch, to whom it is dedicated, and therein lay a tale.

I encountered Heribert's first book, *In Plain Sight: Felix A. Sommerfeld, Spymaster in Mexico, 1908 to 1914*, in Thailand in the fall of 2014. I have had a long and abiding interest in Mexico, its press and the Revolution (1910 to 1920). I realized Heribert was doing the best research on the Mexican Revolution I had seen in years. We began an e-mail conversation that continues to this day. I read his next two books, *The Secret War on the United States in 1915*, and *Felix A. Sommerfeld and the Mexican Front in the Great War*, and had the privilege, along with Rosa King, of editing *The Secret War Council: The German Fight Against the Entente in America in 1914*.

I did not meet Heribert in person until March 2016, when he came to Albuquerque on a book promotion tour in conjunction with the centennial of Pancho Villa's raid on Columbus, New Mexico, which may have been instigated by Felix Sommerfeld. I got to see Heribert give an incredible presentation and we spent four days, talking almost non-stop.

At one point, I asked Heribert how Sommerfeld viewed Pancho Villa, and Heribert responded, "I think Sommerfeld viewed him as somewhat of a brute."

Few Americans know the Mexican Revolution, or, for that matter, World War I, as well as Heribert, but this answer set my monkey mind off. How much do we accept in history that reflects the mindset of historians?

I have known the work of Ricardo Flores Magón since the 1980s, when I wrote a master's thesis in journalism at the University of Montana on Porfirio Díaz and the press. I did not read any of his work translated into English until I undertook this book. I was taken with him as a writer, but accepted the routine version of his place in the history of the Mexican Revolution: A wild-eyed radical who continued to move crazily to the left, dismissed and glorified as an anarchist. Flores Magón was, the historians said, basically a propagandist. Between 1987 and my meeting with Heribert, I spent 20 years in Indian country as both a journalist and a teacher. As a teacher, I taught the Crow and Navajo Nations, and spent years as a reporter covering tribal government. I got to know the people and their cultures.

I also spent decades outside the United States, reading newspapers in foreign countries that were often bought and paid for propaganda and looked at US news through the filter of distance. I was the first American copy editor at the *Shenzhen Daily* in China, and became interested in comparative journalism while teaching in Nigeria.

I knew how newspapers worked. At 22 I was the youngest editor in Montana, and then spent my formative years in the underground press. Still, Heribert's statement brought me up short. I hold a BA in English (with a history minor) and a Master's degree in journalism. I have more college credits in history than any other discipline. However, Heribert changed the way I look at history and historians. He is a very careful man and proved with his own work that less diligent historians can get it absolutely wrong. Ricardo Flores Magón became the focus of our conversation and just as Pancho Villa might have been too brutish for Felix Sommerfeld and Woodrow Wilson ("we will teach those Latins to elect good men), Ricardo Flores Magón was too left wing for historians to accept for who he was and what he did. For four days, Heribert and I batted the subject back and forth, and the idea of this book was born.

This is not a biography of Ricardo Flores Magón. For that, I would recommend *The Return of Comrade Flores Magón* by Claudio Lomnitz or *Always a Rebel: Ricardo Flores Magón and the Mexican Revolution* by Ward S. Albro. Nor is it a collection of his works. For that I would recommend *Dreams of Freedom: A Ricardo Flores Magón Reader*, edited and translated by Chaz Bufe and Mitchell Cowen Verter. While I cite these works often, I turned to Ricardo Flores Magón himself more often, thanks to the Digital Archives of Ricardo Flores Magón at http://archivomagon.net/periodicos/regeneracion-1900-1918/1ra-epoca/.

That site also contains at least some of his correspondence, which is both substantial and illuminating.

I realized in my conversations with Heribert in March 2016, that history is often, as Felix Sommerfeld himself put it when federal agents arrested him for being a German national (they didn't have a clue about his true life as a naval intelligence agent), "a long and convenient memory."

This is the story of a very good writer who has been dismissed as a propagandist, or rallied behind as a great anarchist agitator. In the end, he was a good newspaper man who began and ended his career simply telling the truth, as he saw it.

Thank you, Heribert.

Introduction

The Mexican Revolution (1910 to 1920) was the bloodiest confrontation that ever occurred in this hemisphere. At the beginning of the decade, 11 million people lived in Mexico. By the end of the decade, a million or more had been killed and a million or more had run away to the United States. The roots of that violence run deep, all the way back to the Spanish *Conquistadores* and Spain's creation of virtual slave states throughout Latin America. When Cortez sacked Tenochtitlán in 1521 and began its transformation to become Mexico City, historians believe the Aztecs ruled over a confederation of 17 million people, and there were as many as eight million more people not affiliated with them. By the time, Miguel Hidalgo launched his ill-fated *Grito de Dolores* in 1810, that number had been reduced to about one million *Indios*.

Of course, that, in itself, is a lie. *Indio* is largely an economic, not a racial description, and then as now, being an Indian in Mexico is an unhealthy proposition.

Associated Press reporter Mark Stevenson wrote in 2001:

> The treatment of Mexico's Indians has been largely an invisible issue for decades.
> Mexicans - most of whom are varying shades of mixed Indian and European ancestry, and who often are themselves the victims of discrimination in the United States - view racism as a foreign phenomenon.
>
> "There isn't any racism in Mexico because we have no blacks," goes a common saying that ignores several realities, including Mexico's small Afro-Caribbean population.

1

For decades, Mexico's 10 million Indians have been revered in textbooks and government propaganda - and systematically ignored.

In 2016, the same reporter wrote:

Chiapas is Mexico's poorest state. On Monday, the World Bank reported that, overall, indigenous people across Latin America continue to suffer from poverty and exclusion, with the wealth gap widening between the indigenous and the rest of Latin American society.

According to government statistics, while about 46 percent of Mexicans were living in poverty in 2014, the number in Chiapas is some 76 percent.

On December 7, 2014, Richard Marosi reported in the *Los Angeles Times*:

- Many farm laborers are essentially trapped for months at a time in rat-infested camps, often without beds and sometimes without functioning toilets or a reliable water supply.

- Some camp bosses illegally withhold wages to prevent workers from leaving during peak harvest periods.

- Laborers often go deep into debt paying inflated prices for necessities at company stores. Some are reduced to scavenging for food when their credit is cut off. It's common for laborers to head home penniless at the end of a harvest.

- Those who seek to escape their debts and miserable living conditions have to contend with guards, barbed-wire fences and sometimes threats of violence from camp supervisors.

- Major US companies have done little to enforce social responsibility guidelines that call for basic worker protections such as clean housing and fair pay practices.

Things change slowly if at all in Mexico, and the reports of mistreatment of Indian laborers have not changed a great deal since John Kenneth Turner's *Barbarous Mexico* began appearing in chapter form in the *American Magazine* in 1909. Being or not being *Indio* in Mexico depends most on the size of your bank account than on the color of your skin.

The carnage of "the Wind that swept Mexico"[1] can be laid at the feet of two men, who eventually became its victims, and both of whom are misunderstood to this day. The irony is these men were more *Indio* than European. One spent his life trying to distance himself from his roots, the other, in a sense, embraced them.

Both Porfirio Díaz and Ricardo Flores Magón were born in Oaxaca - Díaz in 1830 to Creole/Mixtec parents (some historians assert that his mother was part Japanese) - Flores Magón in 1873 or 1874 as the middle son of a creole mother and Zapotec father.[2] In his own time, Porfirio Díaz was lauded as the maker of modern Mexico. But his fate would have him leave Mexico in disgrace as an old man. Ricardo Flores Magón – who lit the fire that burned Mexico down – had a more unpleasant end and has been discarded as a propagandist for the anarchist cause. Neither version is quite complete.

Porfirio Díaz was a man of his time, and it was a harsh time – especially in Mexico. In the annals of Mexican villainy, Díaz ranks second only to Victoriano Huerta, the man responsible for Francisco Madero's death. Díaz began as a

---

[1] The name of a book on the Mexican Revolution written by Anita Brenner in the 1940s.

[2] Researchers and biographers are evenly split between the two birth years.

"liberal" and a protégé of Benito Juarez, who is a veritable saint in Mexican mythology. Díaz came to power in 1876, with the ironic slogan of "*Sufragio Efectivo, No Reelección.*" Díaz was to modern Mexico what Mao Tse-tung was to modern China. Like Mao, Díaz was able to unify his county and push it toward modernity, and although he became the darling of the US press, he faced some harsh criticism along the way. *El Tiempo*, a newspaper friendly to the Catholic Church, wrote in 1888 that his reign was one of "tyranny, most cruel and odious."[3] Just as his administration moved Mexico toward the future, he also was the prime motivator of the 20th century Mexican newspaper industry, and he learned how to control that industry, albeit brutally.

Ricardo Flores Magón's legacy underwent significant challenges in the years since his death. In *La Capitol: A biography of Mexico City*, Jonathan Kendall dismissed the Flores Magón brothers as pamphleteers. "These dissidents," he wrote, "hardly posed a threat to Díaz, but their writings ended the political silence that had marked the country since the 1880s."[4] The Flores Magón brothers were hardly alone in their dissent – Díaz managed to fill the infamous Belen prison with journalists, as both economics and technology changed the nature of that industry in Mexico in the 1890s. As for his adventures in the United States, in an otherwise excellent book, *The Plan de San Diego: Tejano Rebellion, Mexican Intrigue*, Harris and Sadler specifically chide Ricardo Flores Magón for not crossing the border when the Revolution broke out in 1910. "Flores Magón was a thinker, not a fighter. The one area where the *Magonistas* excelled was propaganda."[5]

---

[3] As quoted in Roeder, Ralph, *Hacia el México Moderno: Porfirio Díaz*, Volume II (México: Fonda de Cultura Económica, 1973), p. 7 (translation by author).
[4] Kendall, Jonathan, *La Capital: A Biography of Mexico City* (New York: Henry Holt and Company, 1990), p. 392.
[5] Harris, Charles H., Sadler, Louis R., *The Plan de San Diego: Tejano Rebellion, Mexican Intrigue* (Lincoln: University of Nebraska Press, 2013), p. 22.

While their own research pinned the blame of the *Plan de San Diego* - which called for all adult gringos older than 16 to be executed and the territory ceded to the United States in 1848 returned to Mexico - on Venustiano Carranza, many historians labeled it a *Magonista* plot. The irony of this is that *Magonista* is a word that Flores Magón would not have used.

In a 1917 play *"Víctimas y Verdugos,"* which Ricardo Flores Magón wrote, the hero confronts a judge for throwing his female companion and aging mother onto the street, noting that the bourgeoisie perverted the ideals of "justice" and "rights" by their own avarice-driven motives. The judge demands:

> "Are you an Anarchist?" to which the hero responds: "I am a friend of justice, of human justice, of the justice that is not written in the codes, of justice that prescribes that all human beings have the right to live without exploiting and without being exploited, without being ordered." The judge yelled, "This man is a *Magonista!*" to which the hero responds: "I am not a *Magonista*; I am an anarchist. An anarchist does not have idols."[6]

Mitchell Cowen Verter, who, according to his co-editor Chaz Bufe, was the main translator of the writings of Ricardo Flores Magón into English, translated the play.

Verter makes an important point about Flores Magón: Ricardo and those who worked closely with him detested the term *Magonista*.

The late historian Friedrich Katz also chimed in, claiming that Ricardo Flores Magón was not as important as Silvestre Terrazas, editor of the *El Correo* in Cuidad de Chihuahua.

---

[6] Bufe, Chaz and Verter, Mitchell Cowen, eds., *Dreams of Freedom: a Ricardo Flores Magón Reader* (Canada: AK Press, 2006), p. 16.

Unlike the *Magonistas*, Silvestre Terrazas never called for a revolution to overthrow the regime, although in 1910, he was quite sympathetic to the Madero revolution. Nevertheless, his paper, because it was legal and had a large and steadily increasing circulation in Chihuahua, played a greater role in galvanizing opposition to the regime than did the Flores Magón and *Regeneración*. In fact, in 1910, Luis Terrazas to a large degree attributed the paternity of the revolution to the agitation of his distant cousin.[7]

It has been written repeatedly that the *Partido Mexicano Liberal* in general, and the Flores Magón brothers in particular, presented no real threat to Díaz. The old man himself knew better. Sometimes it is hard to see through the haze of history, but two things remain crystal clear: Porfirio Díaz feared Ricardo Flores Magón, and Ricardo Flores Magón hated Porfirio Díaz.

---

[7] Katz, Friedrich, *The Life and Times of Pancho Villa* (Stanford: Stanford University Press, 1998). Dr. Katz cited secondary sources: Wasserman, Mark, *Capitalist, Caciques, and Revolution: The Native Elite and Foreign Enterprise in Chihuahua, Mexico, 1854- 1911* (Chapel Hill: University of North Carolina Press, 1984) and Lloyd, Jane-Dale, *El Proceso de Modernización Capitalista en el Noroeste de Chihuahua* (Mexico: Universidad Iberoamericana, 1987).

Chapter 1
Porfirio Díaz and the Press

We needed a man, a conscience, a will to unify our moral forces and transmute them into normal progress; this man was Porfirio Díaz.

Justo Sierra[8]

There are no monuments to Porfirio Díaz in Mexico City, no streets or institutions named after him. However, near the *Paseo de la Reforma* the monolithic structures that house the largest newspapers in Mexico, *El Universal* and *Excélsior*, can be said to be part of his legacy.

Porfirio Díaz, one of the first victims of the Mexican Revolution, had been the focal point of a public relations program ahead of its time. The foreign press, especially in the United States, found the old man made good copy. Grey-haired and dignified, he posed in his uniform and was more often referred to as "general" than "president." Díaz had displayed military prowess against the French during the War of Intervention, but his real genius lay in his astute political and organizational abilities. During his dictatorship, he was called both "The Maker of Modern Mexico" and the greatest statesman of his time. For 20 years after his fall from power in 1911, he was vilified in the controlled press he helped to create.

---

[8] Sierra, Justo, *The Political Evolution of the Mexican People,* translated by Charles Ramsdell (Austin: University of Texas Press, 1969), p. 366.

Porfirio Díaz rose from the chaos of political instability in nineteenth century Mexico. His parents were not wealthy. He also was not, as an American feature writers for the *New York Times* insisted, completely Creole (Mexican-born Spaniards). He was *Mestizo* (Indian-Spanish). While he did not emphasize that part of his heritage, it gave him an advantage when dealing with other *Mestizos*.

Porfirio Díaz. Courtesy Library of Congress, LC-B2- 774-10 [P&P]

Like many leaders of Mexico, Díaz received his primary education from the Catholic Church. The priest who taught him hoped he would join the clergy, but Díaz opted for a more lucrative career in law. He became embroiled in the *Plan de Ayutla* revolt in 1854, the revolt that brought Benito Juárez to power. From then on, he was a soldier, rising swiftly through the ranks.

Díaz was not a brilliant tactician, but from the beginning he showed keen organizational abilities. In his first assignment under Benito Juárez, who was intermittently president of Mexico between 1858 and his death in 1872, Díaz organized a national guard of 400 Indians in his native state of Oaxaca, a force sufficient to ensure that the state did not stray too far from the Juárez government. Díaz left the army to serve in the Mexican Congress in 1861, but returned to the military to quell a revolt of conservatives. For this, he was promoted to the rank of brigadier general. On returning to Congress he saw his victory dismissed as a matter of small importance. Some historians blame his contempt for parliamentarians on this experience.

During the war of the French Intervention, 1859-1867, Díaz returned to arms, distinguishing himself at the Battle of Puebla in 1866 and as the first military commander to re-establish Mexican control over the capital. Although Juárez, Díaz' mentor, regained control of the government, small rebellions were rife in Mexico and wealthy individuals controlled much of the country. Díaz left the military once more in 1868 and was nominated a candidate in the 1870 elections against Juárez.

During this period, the Mexican press, lacking both modern technology and a literate audience, communicated only with the elite. While political broadsides were common, these were never intended for the masses. The industry began to grow in the 1860s and much of this fledgling press supported the Díaz nomination, operating under the freedom of the press guaranteed by the 1857 constitution.

When Juárez won the elections, the press questioned both the integrity of the ballot count and the idea of self-perpetuation in office. Newspapers helped spread *Porfirista* propaganda to the elites throughout the country. Many of Díaz' amiable relationships with members of the press, including key figures in the opposition press, date from this period.[9]

On November 8, 1871, Díaz led a revolt against Juárez. In *Plan de la Noria* he charged, "the indefinite, forced and violent re-election of the Federal Executive has placed the national institutions in danger."[10] The revolt failed, and Díaz became a fugitive in his own country for several months. After the unexpected death of Juárez in 1872, Díaz was granted amnesty and remained a political force. His second uprising, announced in the *Plan de Tuxtepec* in 1876, succeeded when he drove Sebastian Lerdo de Tejada, successor to Juárez, into exile and assumed the presidency, still using what would prove to be the ironic battle cry of "No re-election!"

Díaz achieved power on a yet-to-crest wave of popularity at the same time the newspaper industry began its period of largest growth in Mexico. Like the wealthy and educated liberals who flocked to serve in the Porfirian administration, the newspapers coalesced, by and large, around Díaz in 1876. He reinforced his popularity when he voluntarily "stepped down" at the end of his first term in 1880.

As Díaz rose to power, events in his home state of Oaxaca profoundly changed his life and Mexico. Teodoro Flores, a Zapotec Indian, had met Margarita Magón at the Battle of Puebla, and they became a couple. It was the second marriage for both, and Margarita would bear three of Teodoro's sons: Jesús in 1871, Ricardo in 1873 or 1874 and

---

[9] Magnor, James A., *Men of Mexico* (Freeport: Books for Libraries Press, 1942), p. 450; *Diario del Hogar*, April 23, 1893.
[10] Reprinted in *Tomos de Su Historia, La Revolución Mexicana,* Tomo I, 1985, p. 9.

Enrique in 1877. Historians give both dates for Ricardo. He claimed he was born on September 16, 1873 – quite a few patriotic Mexican claimed to be born on the Independence Day of Mexico, including Filomeno Mata who also is important to this story. Díaz himself claimed September 15, 1830 as his birthday.

The boys were born into a rapidly changing Mexico, and they would change with it. Both Jesús and Ricardo in later life became lawyers. However, they spent their childhoods in the communal life of the Zapotecs. In their young adulthood, the boys became stylish young political renegades in the nation's capital. This period was transitional for them, especially, for Ricardo and Enrique. Their father instilled in them an appreciation of the communal ways of his tribe, even though his own political contacts lured the family into the Mexican capital in the late 1880s or early 1890s.[11]

Díaz was changing Mexico. The period between Mexican Independence and his ascension to power had been one of political instability and economic stagnation. It saw the rise of the powerful *Hacendados,* the powerful elite who basically put Díaz into power and kept him there. Díaz improved the economy by inviting foreign investment, allowing the construction of railroads, but he also used the laws created in during the Lerdo regime – aimed at confiscating Church land – to disenfranchise Indian tribes and land, subjecting many Indians to the debt peonage of southern Mexico. Enrique, in particular, seemed to be fascinated with the plight of his fellow Indians, and often wrote about it. Ricardo Flores Magón is now considered a hero of the Mexican Revolution, but is remembered outside of Mexico – if at all – as an anarchist. Hence, the vast

---

[11] The precise date of the family moving is unknown, however on May 16, 1892, when the Flores-Magón family was well-established in Mexico City, all three brothers took part in a massive protest in the capital. Both Jesús and Ricardo were arrested. Ricardo was released because if his age. Jesús spent a year in prison.

majority of his work that has been translated and published is from 1910 to 1918. The real impact of the Flores Magón brothers came long before that. There is no doubt that Ricardo Flores Magón died an anarchist, but it was his upbringing as much as anything that would put him at odds with Porfirio Díaz. Enrique alluded to this much later when he was asked if he and Ricardo read Marx. He replied, they did not. They read the anarchist writers because "the works reaffirmed the traditions of our tribe."[12]

Díaz relinquished the presidency in 1880 to Manuel Gonzales, but most historians believe he intended already then to return to power in 1884, which he did. During the term of Gonzales, Mexican law concerning the press changed considerably because Díaz, after a short stint as governor of Oaxaca, returned to Mexico City to serve as the chief justice of the Mexican Supreme Court. The Mexican government tried to ensure the docility of the press through subsidies and a government monopoly on newsprint. The *New York Times* noted that opposition newspapers suffered from government persecution in Mexico as early as 1883. As chief justice, Díaz ruled that judges could hear appeals concerning bail they themselves had set for defamation offenses, which were criminal, not civil matters according to the 1857 constitution. He also ruled that it was legally proper for a judge to consider an *amparo* (defense) concerning a defamation case over which the same judge had ruled. *Amparos* were injunctions against the government for the loss of constitutional rights, and an important part of Mexican law. The loftiest ideals of Mexican journalism are found in these briefs, but little of its history.[13]

The last days of the Gonzales administration further strengthened judicial power when the constitution was amended to eliminate the two-jury system used in

---

[12] Roeder, *Hacia el México moderno, Volumen II,* p. 248.
[13] Baker, Richard D, *Judicial Review in Mexico: A study of the Amparo Suit* (Austin: University of Texas Press, 1971), p. 111.

defamation cases. According to the constitution, one jury determined guilt, another punishment. Under the amendment, no juries were involved – government judges were given both responsibilities. Mexican journalists responded by calling for lifetime judicial appointments to break the tie between government and judges, but to no avail.[14]

In practice, legalities were of little concern to Díaz, who, it is said, developed a simple three-step method to deal with out-of-line journalists. He would bribe them, then jail them, and then kill them.

But defamation laws were not the only legal structures in need of change to accommodate the Díaz regime. The Constitution of 1857 was changed to allow for the re-election of Díaz in 1888, then amended before each national election until 1910. Most Mexicans were probably relieved because since 1848 not one president had completed a term in office until Díaz was elected.

In the beginning, Díaz, by his own admission, used brutality to gain social order. If a *jefe* (political boss) of a district was dispatched to capture a criminal and failed, the *Jefe* suffered the punishment for the crime. Simple highway robbery brought the death penalty. "We endured," Díaz later said, "even through cruelty. But it was all necessary for the life and progress of the nation. If we have been cruel, the ends justified the means."[15]

Díaz knew his countrymen responded to personalities and recognized the necessity for an *amigo* or more accurately an *amigo de caudillo* (friend of the boss) system of

---

[14] Sandals, Robert Lynn, "Silvestre Terrazas, the Press and the Origins of the Mexican Revolution in Chihuahua," doctoral dissertation (Portland: Department of History, University of Oregon, 1967), pp. 59-50; De Fornaro, Carlo, *Díaz, Czar of Mexico* (New York: self-published, 1901), p. 95.

[15] Interview with Porfirio Díaz by James Creelman, *Pearson's Magazine*, 1908, as quoted in *La Revolución Mexicano, Textos de su Historia* (México: Secretaria de Educación Pública, 1985), p. 22.

government. In Porfirian Mexico, the governors owed their power to the president, the *jefe politicos* to the governors and so on down to village structures. For all its structure, the system was chaotic: Díaz encouraged bickering so he could rise above it, granting favors, and gaining loyalty. He fulfilled a need on the part of the *Mestizos* who craved power by appointing members of that segment of society to positions that would provide not only salaries and power but opportunities for graft, illegal seizures of property from *campesinos,* and other forms of self-enrichment. The large *haciendas* were left intact, and concessions extended to industrial activities. In fact, some *haciendas* were enlarged, and owned by foreigners as Díaz actively sought foreign investments, particularly in mining and railroads.[16]

Life improved for a portion of the Mexican population during the *Porfiriato*, particularly in Mexico City. There was a growing middle class which created a market for consumer goods. In 1882, Filomeno Mata started *Diario Del Hogar*, a five-day a week daily that printed four pages, and could boast as much as a twenty-five percent advertising load. These advances were attributed to Díaz, who had opened the country to foreign investment by imposing a system that ensured stability. Ironically, the three advances that Díaz himself took the most pride in − the development of the railroad system, the growth of an urban middle class and the advance of education − played significant roles in his own downfall. When Díaz became president, there were only 578 kilometers of rail lines in all of Mexico. By 1909, there were 24,160. Díaz believed, as journalist Manuel de Zamacona wrote in the early days of the *Porfiriato*, that "Railroads will resolve all the political, social and economic problems which patriotism, sacrifice and the blood of two generations has failed to settle."[17]

---

[16] Hanson, Roger D., *The Politics of Mexican Development* (Baltimore: John Hopkins University Press, 1984), pp. 150-155.
[17] Godoy, Francisco, *Porfirio Díaz, Presidente de México, El Fundador de una Gran República* (Mexico: Muller, 1910), p. 42.

Ultimately, foreigners completed and funded the railroads, which were needed to ship mineral ore to the smelters in the United States. Many Mexicans resented this investment, including journalists. Mining had been a substantial factor in Mexico since the days of the *Conquistadores* and silver and copper was a major export. In fact, Mexican silver was abundant enough that the Mexican peso was a world-wide currency, used extensively in far off China. But the largest copper mines in northern Mexico were owned by foreigners. In this conflict, Díaz was caught in the middle. While it would have been political suicide not to pay homage to Mexican paranoia concerning foreign powers, the economic well-being of the Díaz regime depended on them. Foreign investments paid the vast construction costs of the railroads, amounting to 20,000 pesos per kilometer in the mountainous areas. Costs were less in the desert, but rarely within the 6,000 pesos-per-kilometers subsidy provided by the Mexican government.[18]

Not only foreigners benefited from the railroads. By 1910, Mexican merchants paid about one-twentieth of what they had paid in transportation costs in 1876. Clothing stores were mainstay advertisers in Mexico City dailies. Although the nouveau riche of the capital followed the fashions of New York and Paris, Díaz found American imperialism a safe propaganda target. He was quoted as saying (although detractors claim he did not have the wit), "Poor little Mexico, so far from God, so close to the United States." In 1905, when Díaz had the government buy a controlling interest in the Mexican Central railroads, it was the most important line in Mexico and the first link in the exclusively American dream of connecting all of South America to the United States by rail. The purchase of the railroad probably alienated some important US based support, but the real problems of the railroads for the *Porfirian* power structure

---

[18] Hanson, p. 19.

had already been created with the emerging first large labor unions in Mexico.[19]

The railroads provided both advertising revenue and a means of delivery for Mexican newspapers. Ironically, both *Diario Del Hogar* and the editions of *Regeneración*, the revolutionary newspaper printed in the United States (while it was in St. Louis), had standing advertisements from the railroads.

It was, however, the *Porfirista* commitment to education that provided publishers with a growing market. The number of school teachers increased, demonstrating that education was a long-standing goal of the Díaz regime. Said Minister of Finance José Limantour: "Education is the national service of the most importance: it is supreme." To the supporters of *Continuismo*, a stable government depended on a homogeneous people, and that homogeneity could be created through education.   In 1877, there were 4,715 teachers in Mexico. By 1909, that number had tripled.[20]

For a county, in which economics could be measured by the sale of shoe leather, this was an accomplishment, but it also reflected a centrist attitude that had plagued the capital since the days of the Aztecs. The leading educational institution was the University of Mexico (UNAM). Funded to produce educators, Justo Sierra, a Díaz supporter who managed to hold fast to his own ideals during the ethical decline of the *Porfiriato*, molded its philosophy. He wrote in

---

[19] Ibid; *New York Times*, May 21, 1901; Dispatches from consular officials in Mexico City, Dispatch 41, enclosure 1. US Department of State, Record group 59, National Archives: Consul General A. Cottshick to Assistant Secretary of State Robert Bacon, June 22, 1906.
[20] Mancisidor, José, *Historia de la Revolución Mexicana* (México: Costa-Amic Editores, no date), p. 36; Bazant, Milada, *Debate Pedagógico durante El Porfiriato* (México: Secretaria de Educación Pública, 1957), p. 9; Creelman, James, *Díaz, Master of México* (New York: Appleton and Company, 1911), p. 338.

1902: "Mexican social evolution will have been wholly abortive and futile unless it attains the final goal – liberty."[21]

Sierra's students were imbued with the ideals of democracy and then sent out to encounter and become part of the poverty of Porfirian Mexico. Francisco Bulnes described the frustration of these educated men: "This poor man had to be excessively stupid to study for years and earn a salary roughly equivalent to that of a train conductor." The increase in literacy in Mexico created problems beyond the school house. Recognizing the dangers of an educated but unemployed sector of a growing population, the Díaz regime created a make-work bureaucracy.[22]

Díaz himself recognized the problem of the growing bureaucracy but was resigned to it. He once responded to a question concerning bureaucratic costs: "Feed the beast." By the first decade of the 20th century, ten to fifteen percent of Mexico's literate population, which made up about eighteen percent of the fifteen million total population, worked for the government. For the most part, government employees were no better off than school teachers. If they lacked connections in the power structure, all they could expect was meaningless work at low salaries and the criticism of the Mexican populace. Sierra described the Mexican bureaucracy as "that great normal school of idleness which has educated our country's middle class."[23]

Much has been written about the Mexican Revolution simply because it entailed every facet of revolution, from palace coup to social revolution. Díaz and his advisors did not realize that revolutions traditionally begin with the intellectuals of the middle class. That group formed the audience for a growing number of publications in Mexico

---

[21] Reyes, Alfonso, prologue to 1940 edition *Political Evolution of the Mexican People* by Justo Sierra, p. 15; Sierra, p. 368.
[22] Cockcroft, James, "El Maestro de Primaria en la Revolución Mexicana," *Historia Moderna de México*, Volumen VII, April-June, 1967, p. 657.
[23] Hansen, p. 150; Sierra, p. 215.

and the *Porfiriato* roughly coincided with what historians of Mexican journalism labeled "the great period of development." Sporadic and influenced by the government, this development had more to do with economics of the newspaper industry than the growth of freedom of the press in Mexico. The increase in journalistic endeavors reflected socio-economic changes in Mexico under Díaz. The mechanics of that industry were largely defined by the statutory law that negated freedom of the press guaranteed in the 1857 constitution.[24]

That article 7 was a reaction to the repressive Lerdo Laws of 1853. During Santa Anna's last attempt to rule Mexico, his advisors determined an independent press represented too great a threat to the stability of Mexico and devised a subsidy system whereby a newspaper had to be linked to the government to exist. Article 7 guaranteed freedom of the press (even with the amendments) unless a publication infringed on private life or threatened public safety. The Porfirian regime simply manipulated the press, especially in Mexico City.[25]

The Porfirian concern with the press was two-fold and sometimes contradictory. First, Díaz and his administration recognized the growing political influence of the popular press on the national politics of Mexico. Díaz had seen the freedom of the press grow under Juárez, and he had seen that freedom used to the detriment of that reformist leader, and even more of Sebastian Lerdo. Lerdo truly believed in the freedom of the press and in 1872 issued the following manifesto:

> ...the freedom of the press, which protects and defends the others, will be inviolable for me as if it was, without exception, in the protracted period

---

[24] Ugarte, José Bravo, *Periodistas y Periódicos Mexicanos* (México: México Heroico Editorial, 1966), pp. 77-81; *Correo de Chihuahua*, January 1, 1899.
[25] Sierra, p. 229.

during which I functioned as a minister for the illustrious President [Juárez] whose loss we lament ... of the excesses which the press may commit, the best corrective is the press itself, enlightened, free, the echo of all opinions and all parties.[26]

The industry grew from a few publications read by an elite minority to eighty-four publications in Mexico City alone in 1881, many of which were aimed at the growing ranks of middle-class Mexico. Díaz wanted that developing power to continue operating on his behalf as it had against Lerdo. Lerdo remained true to his word until the last month of his regime when, in desperation, he suspended freedom of the press, which he explained in a government circular pointing out that the press "had declared itself openly revolutionary and subversive." Unknowingly, Lerdo set a dangerous precedent. [27]

Undoubtedly, the Mexican press under Lerdo helped sweep Díaz into power. Some of the important newspapers in this struggle, such as *El Monitor* and *El Ahuizote*, would be repressed by Díaz. For the most part, he would use existing laws to suppress the press. Under Mexican law, journalists were liable if they published articles that produced criminal consequences. Because of basic Porfirian alterations of the law, they also became liable for the articles that *might* produce criminal consequences. In 1885, the courts devised the *psicología*, a test in which a journalist's attitude toward the regime was judged. If he had an attitude considered dangerous to society, he could be jailed.[28]

Díaz recognized the importance of the press in terms of public relations, which could influence foreign relations. When he assumed the presidency, Mexico's image was that

[26] Kapp, Frank Averill, Jr., *The Life of Sebastian Lerdo de Tejada, 1823-1899: A study of Influence and Obscurity* (New York: Greenwood Press, 1968), p. 223.
[27] Ibid, p. 232.
[28] Sandals, pp. 51-52.

of a country not able to guarantee the safety of foreign investments because of political instability.

Porfirian interests were served not only by creating a positive image of Díaz himself, but by portraying Mexico as a "sister republic" of the United States. This was often difficult to do, as illustrated by the case of A. A. Cutting in 1886. He was an American journalist who published *El Centinela* in El Paso del Norte, the town that would eventually be renamed Ciudad Juarez. When the Mexican Emilio Medina began a rival newspaper, Cutting placed an ad in the *El Paso Herald*, saying that Medina's purpose was to "swindle advertisers." Cutting printed cards reiterating the charges, both in English and in Spanish and handed them out on both sides of the border. Accustomed to the accepted practice of lambasting one's editorial opponents common on the American frontier, Cutting included one card that claimed Medina was a "Fraud and deadbeat."[29]

Cutting was arrested in Mexico and jailed in Ciudad de Chihuahua. He refused to recognize the validity of Mexican law and appealed to the American consulate in El Paso del Norte. When Medina heard about it, he assaulted the consulate and was arrested on a weapons charge. Cutting tried to bribe the guards to place Medina in his cell.

The incident, which Díaz later called "something of no importance in itself," created unforeseen tensions along the border. The Mexican government increased the number of troops stationed in Ciudad Juarez from 200 to 2,000. At one point, the Mexican judiciary offered Cutting his freedom on bail, but he refused, saying "I'm under the protection of my government."[30]

The US Government, though, did not want to get involved, much to the ire of the *New York Times*, which editorialized:

---

[29] *New York Times*, July 25, 1886.
[30] Ibid; Dispatches from Mexico City, 1822-1906, US Department of State, Record Group 59, National Archives: Consulate translations of Díaz speech to Mexican Congress, Sept. 6, 1886.

"The best proof of the worthlessness of Mexico is the fact that we have not annexed any part of that country since the treaty that closed the Mexican war." [31] Several days after that editorial appeared, Mexicans killed a Mexican-American accused of being a horse-thief. The *Times* ran the story under the headline: "Texans will Protect American Citizens even if Uncle Sam Won't."

A week later, the judges in Chihuahua, who had made it known they known they would "brook no interference from the US government or, for that matter, Díaz himself," found Cutting guilty, sentenced him to a year in jail and fined him $600. After the public lost interest, Cutting was freed and quietly slipped across the border.[32]

The *New York Times* reported that "Medina, who had caused all the trouble, has leave to sue Cutting." The *Times* turned around, though, and editorialized that perhaps the case had two sides. It would be a long time before Mexican press law would again be questioned in the US press.[33]

Antagonism between the government and the small press in Mexico bloomed with the 1888 re-election of Díaz and the constitutional amendment allowing that re-election. By then, the power structure of the *Porfiriato* was in place and the style entrenched. In the early June, Díaz began receiving letters from state governors advising him that an uncontrolled press would damage Mexico. An unfavorable article had been reprinted in Havana, Cuba, and the *Porfiristas* feared that some of the bad publicity would creep into the US and European press.[34]

The governor of Jalisco recommended jailing three of the worst offenders in that state, and in Chihuahua, the

---

[31] *New York Times*, July 28 and August 1, 1886.
[32] Ibid, August 8,1886; Valadez, José C., *El Porfirismo: Historia de un Régimen* (México, DF: Editorial Patriar, 1946), p. 146.
[33] Ibid, August 15, 1886.
[34] Personal archives of Porfirio Díaz, 1876-1916, Universidad Iberoamericana, file number 006102, (unsigned, undated), 00648 (Romaron Carnova to Díaz, June 30, 1888).

governor jailed the author of a letter to the editor. The Chihuahua governor explained in a letter to Díaz that one writer could result in "grave danger" to society (Díaz made a note to commend the governor for his positive action).[35]

From all sides, Díaz was being told that the persecution of journalists was justified to ensure the order and tranquility of the country. By the end of the summer, Díaz received several more letters from state governors, saying they had jailed journalists and publishers. Many of the letters contained pleas for harsher laws to deal the opposition press.[36]

These laws were not forthcoming. Díaz and his administrators recognized the mechanisms for controlling the press were already in place. There were also extra-legal procedures for dealing with troublesome journalists, such as assassination, but the outright killing of newspapermen was not common. Francisco Bulnes wrote that only five journalists were killed during the *Porfiriato* and those murders were ordered by state governors not federal administrators. That number has been disputed recently by historians (and does not count a number of journalists who died from disease in Belen or afterwards). The *Porfiristas* preferred incarceration to elimination. Díaz himself recognized that a repentant journalist was more valuable to *Continuismo* than a martyr, and he would sometimes intervene on behalf of journalists if he believed they had "learned their lesson."[37]

During the last ten years of the nineteenth century, the Porfirian system was perfected, and Díaz became the

[35] Ibid, 006519, Governor of Chihuahua to Díaz, July 26, 1888, 006523, Lauro Carrillo to Díaz, marginal note from Díaz, July 26, 1888, 00672 through 00672, unsigned, undated report to Díaz from Coahuila, 006814, Governor of Monterrey to Díaz, August 27, 1888.

[36] Ibid, 00753 and 07537, Secretario Del Gobernador de Jalisco to Díaz, August 5 and 15, 1988; 0007586, Rafael Cravioto to Díaz, August 27, 1888.

[37] Sandals, pp. 59-60; personal interview with Jane Dale Lloyd, UIA.

unquestioned darling of the press, both domestic and foreign. At age sixty, he had mastered the delicate act of balancing the power structure. Unfortunately, his administration gladly sacrificed the viability of the Mexican press for stability and growth.

Chapter 2

When Old Friends Fight

The 1890s were the "Gilded Age." The images remain: a peaceful Europe was dominated by matriarchy of Queen Victoria, the United States hosted the gala events of the wealthy Robber Barons, and the world's urban centers emulated their demeanor and fashions (if not their wealth). The so-called *Cientificos,* who believed that science cured all social ills, administered Mexico. The capital Mexico City hosted a population of about a half million souls, many rich enough and literate enough to support the burgeoning newspaper industry. But not all things were light and gay.

In 1922, writing almost 30 years after serving his first prison term in Belen, Ricardo Flores Magón, described the dark side of Mexico's progress:

> The dungeon was unpaved, and a layer of mud from three to four inches composed the floor, while the walls oozed a turbid fluid which prevent from drying up the expectorations, countless, careless, former occupants had negligently flung upon them. From the ceiling, enormous cobwebs overhung, in which black, horrid spiders lurked. In one corner, opening from the sewer there was a hole [...] my lungs then youthful and healthy could resist the poison of that grave, my nerves, though sensitive, could be trained by my will to respond with nothing more than a slight

tremor to the assaults and bites of the rats in the dark
...[38]

Belen Prison, originally a convent housing sixty nuns was converted into a prison. The Díaz regime used it largely to incarcerate wayward journalists. It was about half the size of a city block and held between 5,000 and 6,000 men, 300 boys and 600 women. Sanitation was almost completely lacking. 176 prisoners died in a single day in 1901; prisoners lingered in dank, subterranean cells without light and only a hole in the corner for a toilet.[39]

After eight days of solitary confinement in these dungeons prisoners could mingle with the general population in the main part of the prison. The prison also had the distinction of having an area known as the "Editor's Room," a special area for journalists who had dared to criticize important officials of the Mexican government. It is said that Filomeno Mata kept a bed there after 1893.[40]

In the spring of that year, Mata, founder, publisher and editor of the *Diario del Hogar*, found himself at odds with the Díaz administration over the persecution of some young journalists. Mata, a contemporary of Díaz, had had an amiable relationship dating from the president's days as a revolutionary. The recent conflicts, that landed Mata in Belen on numerous occasions, once again erupted over the interpretation of the 1857 constitution, especially freedom of the press.

---

[38] Flores Magón as quoted by Henry Weinberger in a letter to the editor, *The New Republic*, July 5, 1922.
[39] De Fornaro, p. 81.
[40] Beals, Carleton, *Porfirio Díaz: Dictator of Mexico* (Philadelphia: JB Lippincott Company, 1932), p. 272.

Filomeno Mata. Creative Commons.

It was a longstanding dispute, as feuds between old acquaintances tend to be. A long-time Mexico City publisher, Mata reflected both the growth of the newspaper industry during the *El Desarrolló Grande de la Prensa* (the great development of the press, 1890-1899) and the economic problems facing the small publishers lacking strong connections with the administration.

Mata began his career in 1869 at the age of twenty-four, working under the tutelage of two established editors, Vincent Garcia Torres of the *El Monitor Republicano* (founded in 1844) and *Ireneo Paz de La Patria* (founded in 1877). These two papers represented the dichotomy of the Mexican Press: *La Patria* became part of the clique Díaz established in 1888. *El Monitor*, conversely, was noted for

27

its tenacity in reporting government misdeeds (including the various incarcerations of Mata). In the beginning, both publishers reflected the optimistic liberalism of the age of reform, as did Mata, who began his professional life as a college professor in San Luis Potosi before being introduced to journalism.[41]

Mata displayed not only optimism but ambition in his youth, founding four different newspapers before launching *Diario del Hogar* in 1881 at age thirty-six. The paper was originally intended as a five-day a week daily for families. Mata had successfully identified the market for the publication as the literate, middle-class Mexican family. The paper sold for five centavos or seventy-five centavos for a month's subscription.[42]

In his first issue, he began the serialization of two novels, one translated for the paper from French. He also favored poetry and recipes – both of which could be hand-set before publication and used as fillers. Mata was more interested in making a living than in espousing political causes. The country seemed politically stable and Mexico City provided not only an audience for Mata's mild publication but also work for his job presses. He accepted a government subsidy. However, a rift with the regime started developing. Criticism of the Catholic Church in Mexico damaged sales and he had to look beyond the family market. Later, during the Gonzales administration, Mata criticized government actions that interfered with journalistic activities. This ended his political non-involvement. He did not, however, oppose the reentry of Díaz to the presidential office in 1884, although he did refuse a government subsidy that year. Throughout most of his career, Mata refrained from attacking Díaz personally in his editorials. Instead, he

---

[41] Beals, p. 267.
[42] Mata, Luis, *Filomeno Mata: su vida y su labor* (México: Secretaria de Educación Pública, 1945), pp. 33-35.

blamed real and imagined wrongs on those who surrounded the president.[43]

The first overt break between Mata and Díaz came on June 22, 1885, when the Díaz government passed a sedition law that prohibited articles damaging to the president or his ministers. The issue was debt owed to Britain. Mata wrote that he would be the first to censor a press that did not do its job, but that he wanted more respect for the basic institutions of society. He prudently drew the line at disrespecting the government but was critical of those governmental activities that "strike at the fundamental laws of the Republic."[44]

When Díaz presented himself as a presidential candidate again in 1888, Mata's editorials opposed the nomination. However, he was careful to level his criticism against the idea of reelection and not Díaz personally. While Mata's editorial attitude towards Díaz as an individual was always tempered, he irrevocably split with the administration over two incidents: the murder of a journalist in Morelia in 1890, and when police sacked his home looking for fugitives. The head of the *Policía Secreta* (also known as the *Bravi*) entered his home, pistol in hand, threatened Mata and accused him of hiding criminals. The Secret police became part of what Mata called "a government that has little love of its people."[45]

Mata was not the first Mexican journalist to find fault with the government, and there were other editors who were more outspoken. But he had widespread connections throughout the small press because of his job printing and over the years, his shop was often responsible, or held responsible, for printing "radical" papers, including *El Demócrata* and *El*

---

[43] Ugarte, p.68.
[44] Ibid; Quiñones, Amada Díaz, *Porfirio Díaz: Los Intelectuales y la Revolución* (México: El Callaíto, 1981), p. 29.
[45] Turner, Ethel Duffy, *Ricardo Flores Magón y el Partido Liberal Mexicana* (México: C.E.N. 1984), p. 19; Mata, pp. 39-49; *Diario Del Hogar*, October 28, 1892.

Hijo de Ahuizote. A wave of protest broke out with the reelection of Díaz in 1892. Many arrests followed. In the early Spring of 1893, the government arrested hundreds of journalists. Headlines decrying the crackdown appeared on the front pages of *Diario del Hogar*. On March 7, 1893, days after the inauguration of Díaz, the government charged Mata and his staff with thirty-seven counts of defamation. He was thrown in jail, but released by March 18, when he again criticized the government in an article headlined, "What is the difference between 1877 and 1893?" The difference, he wrote, was that Mexico now had railroads. Foreigners, he said, built the railroads but Mexico had the debt.[46]

---

[46] Ross, Stanley R., editor, *Fuentes para la historia contemporánea de México: Periódicos y revistas* (México: El Colegio de México, 1965).

Chapter 3

Defending the Next Generation

On April 1, 1893, the government arrested the staff of two publications, *Noventa y Tres* and *El Demócrata*. College students impatient for changes in Mexico had founded and staffed both the year before. On the staff of *El Demócrata* were Jesús and Ricardo Flores Magón, giving both a second introduction to Belen. They had been arrested in a major student protest in 1892. Mata protested the arrest in an editorial. The next day, *Diario* did not appear, and for the next two weeks, the content of the paper was noticeably unpolitical. This became a telling trend in the paper: when Mata was incarcerated at Belen, which happened more than thirty times in 1893 alone, the paper was bereft of any news of radical or press activity. Instead it concentrated on innocuous news, poetry, or the ever-popular cooking recipes.[47]

When Mata was free and working, notices of government malfeasance or press persecution filled the *Boletín* section of his paper. A review of the surviving editions of the paper in the database *World Newspaper Archives* reveals a dearth of missing editions: how much of this resulted from Mata's Belen stints, and how much of it came from a lack of preservation of many Mexican newspapers cannot be determined. Mata was free on April 28 1893, when *Diario* reported the final government closure of *El Demócrata*. The

---

[47] Personal interview with Jane Dale Lloyd; *Diario del Hogar*, April 2, 1893.

31

paper had been closed for a particularly critical piece. Mata responded by quoting it, almost in its entirety. The article began, "Not since the tyranny of Santa Anna. . ." Still, Mata soft-pedaled the responsibility of Díaz. "We don't believe that the president of the Republic, a man who has shown in other times a passion for liberal ideas, gave the order for this persecution." Yet, he did not let Díaz of the hook either: "At the same time, he has not intervened."[48]

The next day Mata continued his verbal barrage, accurately predicting the closure of two more newspapers. Mata, who rarely referred to himself in print, noted that the directors of *El Monitor*, *El Tiempo* and his own paper were free only because they had paid a bond to a Mexico City court as insurance against defamation. He added that he, alone, was responsible for the publication of that particular article in *Diario*. Another prophetic front page article headlined: "Opinion of the press: Near the end." Publication of *Diario* was suspended for five days thereafter.[49]

It was at this point that the lives of Mata and the Flores Magón family began to intersect. Both Jesús and Ricardo had gone to jail in 1892 during the student protests, and Jesús had been one of the founders of *El Demócrata*, which Mata had also defended. Jesús had been sentenced to five months in jail, and his father, Teodore Flores, died just a few days into his incarceration. Described as an idealistic and principled man, Teodore had impressed the importance of Juarez' fight against the oppression of indigenous people upon his sons, a situation that *Porfirista* policy had exacerbated. Unlike the competitive nature of Mexico City, where the three brothers had moved to as teenagers, Teodore rhapsodized about village life in Oaxaca, where there was no need of government officials. Instead each person produced what they could and took what they

---

[48] *Diario del Hogar*, April 28, 1893.
[49] Ibid, April 29, 1983.

needed. Their mother, who idolized Juárez, shared these views.

Yet, she happily moved her family to Mexico so her sons could get the best education. When Teodore died, and Jesús was in jail, supporting the family fell to young Ricardo, who took jobs setting type for several newspapers – given the politics of the time, those papers were probably *Diario Del Hogar* and Daniel Cabrera's *El Hijo de Ahuizote*, both of which were part of the opposition press[50]

El Hijo de Ahuizote. Courtesy Archivo Magón.

The fact that Ricardo learned type setting skills as a young man is of major importance, because that ability was critical and in high demand for publications that could not afford the new Linotype machine. The *New York Times* did not move to this technology until 1894, and many small papers never did.

Meanwhile, Mata was out of Belen again, and, on May 12, urged the government to pass a law that would protect the

[50] Verter, Mitchel Cowen, Bufe, Chaz, eds., *Dreams of Freedom: A Ricardo Flores Magón Reader* (Oakland: AK Press, 2006), pp. 31, 32.

press from the judicial system. The coverage of the journalists incarcerated in Belen continued, and for most of June, Mata joined them. Mata referred to his own incarceration only once, noting dryly, "yes, we have seen the insides of Belen." But other publications covered his adventures with the *Bravi*, especially *El Monitor Republicano*, until the government forced that publication into permanent suspension in 1896. Undoubtedly, because of his relationship with Díaz, Mata received preferential treatment in Belen, at times even being able to write articles inside the prison.[51]

In early July, authorities brought defamation charges against *Diario del Hogar* for the 39th time in 1893. Mata reported the event on July 11 in an article that shared the front page with Belen. Predictably, in the days after those articles, *Diario* concentrated on other news: European events were given a fair amount of play, as were problems in Nicaragua and speeches by US President Grover Cleveland. The elections in the Mexican provinces also received matter of fact reporting. The lack of coverage of persecution indicates that in all probability, Mata was in Belen. He was out by August 22 and brought his readers good news: an amnesty had been suggested for journalists in Belen. Enthusiastically, Mata called the idea "the conquest of right" and praised the government for the move, which he may well have begun in personal correspondence with Díaz. When the amnesty failed to materialize, Mata took a different tack: he ran the names of journalists incarcerated in Belen. For three consecutive days, the list appeared: set in eight-point type with a 14-pica column width, the lists ran 20 inches – totaling 60 inches of names in tiny print. Then, again, the paper became silent on the issue.[52]

---

[51] *Diario del Hogar*, May 2 and 30; personal interview with Jane Dale Lloyd.
[52] Ibid, August 1 through 22, August 31 through September 5, 1893.

A young Daniel Cabrera, Creative Commons.

In late October, Daniel Cabrera, founder and editor or *El Hijo de Ahuizote,* and one of the few men who could claim as much time in Belen as Mata, was arrested. Mata complained in print, "we have had the opportunity to read the article and, frankly, we were surprised at the proceedings because it dealt with a country far away from Mexico." Again, the tone of *Diario* changed for a time.[53]

Both Cabrera and Mata corresponded with Díaz during their stays in prison. The dictator replied that while would like to help them, their fate was out of his hands. He blamed their situation on the attitudes of others in his administration. Throughout his regime, Díaz managed to maintain friendly relations with the great majority of members of the press, even those who were editorially opposed to *Continuismo*. In this, the Flores Magón brothers would prove a major exception – they hated him and he would come to fear them.

---

[53] Ibid, October 27-30, 1893.

The rest of the press accepted the idea that problem was not the man, but the system, and by 1893 the system had almost succeeded in eliminating the opposition press in Mexico. Many of the journalists incarcerated in 1893 did not raise their editorial voices for seven years. Although 1896 is the year many Mexican historians identify as the beginning of the great development of Mexican journalism - marked by the founding of the Cientifico-funded *El Imparcial* and the use of Linotype machines in Mexico - the government had come close to effectively stamping out opinion in the press three years earlier.

Three independent papers were left in Mexico City by 1896: *Diario Del Hogar, El Hijo de Ahuizote* and *El Monitor Republicano.* Perhaps the first two could continue, albeit with frequent jail sentences for their administrators and staffs, because of the publishers' old ties to Díaz. *El Monitor Republicano* was not so fortunate and the government permanently suspended its operation in late 1896. The *Cientifico*-oriented *Monitor* replaced the paper by. Fabian Conde, a staff member responsible for much of the government criticism that appeared in its pages during the late 1890s, chronicled the change in *Diario.* An article headlined "Are there any party politics in Mexico?" praised the old *Monitor* as the "defender of honorable politics, true liberties and the right of the people to know their institutions." The new *Monitor*, Conde predicted, would be nothing more than a vehicle for Cientifico propaganda.[54]

Conde began a series of articles on government journalists in early 1897, referring mainly to the staff of the new *Monitor*, published by Reyes Spindola. In the articles, Conde accused the *Monitor* staff of betraying everything from the constitution of 1857 to the Catholic Church, labeling it counter-revolutionary. "What kind of government would you have us have?" he asked. Mata published an article

---

[54] Sandals, pp. 53, 54, 59; personal interview with Jane Dale Lloyd; *Diario del Hogar*, December 30, 1896 and January 9, 1897.

disclosing the amount of money Spindola received for the *Monitor* alone: a start-up subsidy of $100,000 (Mex.), and annual subsidy of $52,000, as well as advertising revenue and job-printing contracts that amounted to more than $12,000 a month. The publishing business in Porfirian Mexico reflected the status quo: those with connections flourished and those without struggled.[55]

The Porfirian administrators had the press in Mexico City under control, but the same economic conditions that created the market for growth in journalism in the capital were also at play in the provinces where state governors filtered the federal powers. In those areas, where subsidies did not exist and the federal government could not enforce the monopoly on newsprint, the conflict arose between the state governments and the publishers.

There was, of course, a major difference between life in the provinces and life in Mexico City. While individual finances improved in Mexico City, life was getting harder for most of the people in the provinces. *Diario Del Hogar* ran a bulletin column on its front page which, at times, referred to the troubles in the provinces, but for the most part residents of Mexico City had little interest, and little knowledge of the debt peonage going on in the Yucatan of *Valle Nacional,* the growth of haciendas on the back of shrinking communal lands in Indian communities, or the labor conditions in the mining centers to the north.

The new social order created during the Porfiriato made many individuals wealthy because of the government appropriation of communal lands for private benefit, while it also saw lives of many indigenous people shattered. "This,"

---

[55] *Diario del Hogar,* January 26 and February 20, 1897; Ugarte, p. 84; Mata, p. 55.

wrote Jane Dale Lloyd, "was the beginning of the movement."[56]

As Roger D. Hansen pointed out, the precepts of *Continuismo* were relatively simple: ignore those without political power and pay off or liquidate those who were politically active and capable. This meant that Díaz basically ignored thirty-five percent of the Mexican population: those who continued to live as Indians. Hansen also points out that those Indians who left their pueblos and adopted mestizo mores were accepted as mestizos. Díaz unwittingly created the force that would tear Mexico apart.[57]

---

[56] Katz, Friedrich and Lloyd, Jane Dale, *Porfirio Díaz frente al descontento Popular Regional, 1891-1893* (México: Universidad Iberoamericana, 1986), p. 185.
[57] Hansen, pp. 146-147.

Chapter 4

The Revolution of the Word

"…we do not call you to revolution, but to save our country and to begin the measures necessary for our salvation." *Diario Del Hogar*

The three Flores Magón brothers participated in a student anti-government demonstration on May 16, 1892 and were promptly detained. The regime released Enrique and Ricardo, but sentenced Jesús to a term in Belen. Both Jesús and Ricardo studied law, while the younger Enrique would eventually study accounting. However, their focus at the time was being part of what Lomnitz referred to as "the class of '92." These were young people who opposed Díaz because of a sense that they would not get their fair share of the economic expansion of their time.[58]

The Flores Magón were a close-knit family. They had moved from Oaxaca to Mexico City specifically so the boys could have a better education. Their income came from a military pension from the boys' father, Teodore, and some property he owned and rented out in Oaxaca. The government cut off his military pension, probably owing to the destruction of his military papers when his home in Oaxaca was burned and ransacked in a pro-royalist raid that killed his first wife and his parents. He died shortly after Jesús was incarcerated, and the burden of supporting the family shifted

---

[58] Bufe, Verter, *Dreams of Freedom*, pp. 31-32.

to Ricardo. While both Jesús and Ricardo were admitted to the bar in 1895, only Jesús actively practiced law. [59]

Jesús Flores Magón.
Courtesy Library of Congress, LC-B2- 3020-6 [P&P].

The Flores Magón family history is rather murky in the 1890s. Teodore died while Jesús was in Belen, but sources are contradictory about how long Ricardo stayed in prison. All the brothers emulated the styles of the day (clothing habits they would retain throughout their careers) and Jesús and Ricardo helped startup *El Demócrata*, a student publication that the Díaz administration quickly put out of

---

[59] Lomnitz, Claudio, *The Return of the Comrade Ricardo Flores Magón* (New York: Zone Books, 2014), pp. 44-45.

business. The bothers' association with Filomeno Mata also date from this time, although Luis Mata's biography of his father, *Filomeno Mata, Su Vida Y Su labor*, published in 1945 did not mention the relationship with the Flores Magón brothers. The student protest, which introduced the brothers to the world of anti-reelection politics, were not reported outside of Mexico City and its coverage in the Mexico City press was divided between the pro- and the anti- Díaz papers. But both sides chose to ignore the economic condition that spawned the anti-Díaz demonstrations. These were young people from families struggling at the edge of prosperity, and most of the intellectuals who later emerged in the revolution got their start in those demonstrations. The ruthless suppression of the protests hardened the spirit of the young people involved and deepened their commitment.[60]

El Demócrata only lasted three months, but it had a massive impact on both Jesús and Ricardo. Although it did not criticize Díaz directly, it certainly found fault with his administration in terms of inept bureaucracies, privilege and power of foreign investors, and, according to Enrique, it radicalized Ricardo. The paper was popular, and its readership grew in its short life, and from this, Enrique would recall late in life, Ricardo discovered the power of writing.[61]

The real turning point for the Flores Magón family came on August 7, 1900 with the first edition of *Regeneración*. Jesús Flores Magón and Antonio Horeastlas (both with the prefix of "Lic." meaning "lawyer") appeared as publishers on the paper. Although Ricardo had been admitted to the bar in 1895, his name, listed both as one of the three *Directores*, and specifically as the *Administrador*, indicated that he was responsible for the editing. The 16-page publication, printed on both sides of eight A4 pages, billed itself as a "*Periódico*

---

[60] Ibid, 64-65.
[61] Roeder, Ralph, *Hacia el México Moderno, Porfirio Díaz, Volume II* (México: Fundo de Cultura Económica, 1973), pp. 182-183.

Jurídico Independiente" (an independent legal journal). Part of Article seven of the 1857 constitution was quoted on the masthead.[62]

The first front page article began with the statement: "This publication is the product of a heartfelt conviction." In careful language, the headlining story laid out a case against the judiciary, and by its third issue, published on August 23, 1900, *Regeneración* earned plaudits from other publications and publications all over Mexico. The publishers dedicated the last two pages of their 16 page A4 paper to excerpts from these missives. They published compliments from *El Atalaya* in Toluca, *El Monitor de Morelos* in Cuernavaca, *El Correo Español*, *La Liberad de Morelia*, *La Libertad de Guadalajara*, and *El Sol* from that same city, and *La Voz de Nuevo León* in Monterrey.

The focus of the early issues was abuses and failings of the Mexican judicial system. Four-month subscriptions of the paper sold for 1.5 pesos in the capital, and 2 pesos for the Mexican states, as well as 2 pesos for foreign subscriptions. It ran articles on corrupt judges who made questionable decisions, and gave other lawyers the chance to argue their cases in print. Quite often, the legal cases involved government suits against newspapers.

The fifth issue, published on September 7, 1900, began with a first page essay of "The Press and the State." The unsigned article argued that "the work of journalism, like that of medicine, required special talents, and part of that work was to uncover injustice." It went on to predict "The future revolution will be that of the word." In that same issue the Flores Magón brothers outlined the legal difficulties facing

---

[62] What follows, unless otherwise noted, is drawn from Archivo Digital de Ricardo Flores Magón (http://archivomagon.net/periodicos/regeneracion-1900-1918/1ra-epoca), translations by the author.

El Hijo de Ahuizote and the closure of a publication called *Onofroff.*[63]

The next issue (September 15) began with an article headlined "the Press and the Law." It pointed out that the "reforms of May 15, 1883, did not destroy the absolute freedom of the press, sanctioned by the 1857 constitution." Until this point, they had been flying under the Díaz radar. They had obviously garnered wide readership among both lawyers and journalists throughout Mexico, but it had been Díaz himself, serving as chief Justice of the Mexican Supreme Court at the time, who had made those reforms. Letters of support for the editorials from newspapers all over Mexico again filled the last page.

Regeneración did not confine itself to the woes of the press, but also gave legal opinions on labor cases and was intensely critical of the sitting judiciary. Much of its legal critiques were based on the 1957 constitution, and were likely penned by Jesús Flores Magón. Different styles of writing were obvious in the publication. The older brother seemed more given to lengthy legal discourse, while the younger brother favored a pithier approach, as when he wrote about "Corruptelas Judiciales" in the ninth issue -- with many one-sentence paragraphs. In the same issue, there was an article headlined, "No Hay Valor Civil" written in the same style in which emphasis was placed on the "victims of the judiciary." To that writer, probably Ricardo, the solution for fixing the judicial system was simply not that difficult.

One can only imagine the newsroom squabbles that went on between the two brothers. Jesús, the older brother, had launched the publication as a legal journal, hoping to reform the legal system from within. Ricardo became more of a firebrand. Who wrote what can only be ascertained by individual writing styles.

---

[63] Ibíd.

The brothers were in accordance concerning the ongoing judicial battle against Daniel Cabrera's *El Hijo de Ahuizote*, and dedicated four pages of the next issue to a legal brief in its defense -- largely based on the idea that the Constitution had precedence over the reforms of 1883.

By this time, *Regeneración* was not only following court cases that involved the press, but had obviously created contacts with publication across Mexico. It also paid attention to the press that Díaz had created, in its next issue (October 15) when El Universal complained that "in Mexico, professionals cannot preach Democracy because this produces mutiny," the idea was amplified by a front-page essay that concluded, democracy did not produce mutiny, but tyranny did. The publication also noted, on a weekly basis, which journalists had been sentenced to Belen.

The next edition, October 22, took up the case of *El Hijo de Ahuizote* again, with a four-page legal brief, probably composed by Jesús. In that same edition, there was a strange passage, in all caps, that annexation of Mexico was entirely possible in five or ten years. This fed on Mexican paranoia, but it also reflected a life-long fear harbored by all three of the Flores Magón brothers.

On Oct. 31, *Regeneración* led with a two-page report on the discussions going on in *La Camera de Diputados* (one way to get legislators anywhere to read any publication is to write about them), and another small article comparing the Mexican with the foreign press, particularly publications in France and Germany. In Mexico, the press was in a precarious position, the article said, and pointed out that neither in Paris or in Berlin were journalists given prison sentences longer than six months.

By this time, the publication was attracting letters from the editor, mostly from other lawyers, and covering a labor dispute between workers and an American company, The Bonsack Machine Company, but the coverage of this conflict was submitted by other lawyers.

On November 7, *Regeneración* took up the case of public employees who took their complaints to court, and in a long winded legal argument, Jesús (probably) took the time to point out it was not a good idea in a country where power was everything. In the next issue, a list of 23 newspapers across Mexico that had protested the legal system was published, since the staff of *El Hijo de Ahuizote* were in Belen, they did not make the list.

In the November 15th edition, an essay blasting the *Diario Official*, a government publication, and ran an inside story about human trafficking in the Yucatan and some recaps of suppression of the press. "We do not seek justice as mercy," it said, "we see it as an obligation."

In the same edition, for the first time *Regeneración* covered a meeting of the *Cientificos*, and reported the suppression of a newspaper in Hermosillo. *Regeneración* reported it was one of three papers denied admission to *el Círculo de Amigos del Presidente* - the others being *El Tiempo* and *Diario del Hogar*.

There was a business announcement in this edition for a *Litografía Moderna* - perhaps a tradeoff for type setting. Until this issue, Díaz had not been named in the publication, but now they reported the "circle of friends" (from which they had been banned) had discussed a statute of Díaz (una estatua del Gral. Díaz) and suggested it be located outside of a prison.

The next issue announced that Jesús was moving his law office to Calle de Humboldt, 408, and away from the offices of *Regeneración*. Below that was a report of the Club Liberal, meeting in San Luis Potosi.

More importantly, they changed the subhead in the next issue to "*Periódico Independiente de Combate*" printed on New Years' Eve, 1900. first page article explained the thinking. In the next few issues, the publication critiqued Díaz for "too many politics, not enough administration," which was opposite of his claim, and the Church, all the while continuing its coverage of the persecution of the Mexican press and the justice system. The publication was being read by lawyers and members of the "independent press" read the paper nationwide. It regularly published legal opinions from lawyers, as well as bits of news that had been published by smaller papers outside Mexico City.

On January 7, the lead essay under the headline "La Lucha por la libertad" argued that the enemy of liberty was the same as the enemy of progress because it had sold the nation's integrity for dollars. Inside there were notices of publications, *"Free thinking"* of Yucatan and *El Despertador* of Guadalajara.

The following week, the lead essay focused on religion and crime, blaming much of the problems on the "regressive" Catholic religion. The second essay was headlined "The heroic women."

On page fourteen of the January 23, 1901 edition was a short article with the headline "La *Regeneración* no es un Hongo" -- *Regeneración* is not a mushroom, which a local administrator had labeled the publication. Beyond demonstrating the Flores Magón brothers still had a sense of humor, it indicated the publication was beginning to bother the administration.

In its January 31 edition, the lead article dealt with *El Gran Congreso Liberal*, to be held the next week in San Luis Potosí. An article further inside the paper named Ricardo Flores Magón as one of the delegates. Ricardo expressed his gratitude for the honor of being selected in a short note below. The issue also contained several articles about problems in education, one noting that elementary education in the Ciudad of Chihuahua was very expensive, citing a cost of 150,000 pesos as yearly tuition, and yet another article on slavery in the Yucatan.

On February 14 and 15, Ricardo Flores Magón took the time to attend the first congress of all the national liberal clubs of Mexico. Basically, this was a lose assortment of political organizations that were against both *Continuismo* and the power of the Catholic Church. Another journalist who attended that meeting was Filomeno Mata. He considered the meeting one of the most important news stories of the decade. He wrote several editorials concerning the formation and growth of the *Club Liberal Ponciano Arriaga* in January. Camilo Arriaga, an engineer by profession, had called the meeting, and the main concern was the resurgence in power of the Catholic Church in Mexico.

Arriaga organized the meeting in response to statements of a Mexican Bishop in the general assembly of the International Congress of Catholic agencies held in Paris the year before. The priest boasted that under Díaz, clerical economic and political elites had been re-established in Mexico. Of the 50 official delegates to the first meeting, only nine were journalists, but one of the first mandates was for liberal clubs at local levels to produce their own newspapers, a common occurrence for political clubs in Mexico at the time. From these anti-clerical beginnings, the clubs developed into the *Partido Liberal Mexicano*, with small clubs spreading throughout Mexico. These became the first real revolutionary threat to the Porfirian regime.[64]

The event was low key, until Ricardo, supposedly representing a student organization, made a speech denouncing the Díaz administration as "a den of thieves."[65] This extended the reach and popularity of *Regeneración*. On February 26, 1901, *Regeneración* led with the

---

[64] Mata, p. 62; Cockcroft, James D., *Intellectual Precursors of the Mexican Revolution* (Cambridge: Cambridge University Press, 1968), pp. 92-93; Taracena, Alfonzo, *La Verdadera Revolución Mexicana*, (México: Editorial Jus, 1965), p. 61.
[65] Poole, David, editor, *Land and Liberty: Anarchist Influences in the Mexican Revolution – Ricardo Flores Magón*, Second Edition (New York: Christie Books, 2012), e-book, no page.

provocative headline, "naming their candidate." The essay didn't name a candidate, but took broad swipes at Díaz. An article followed naming the liberal clubs in 14 states and their officers.

Club Liberal Ponciano Arriaga. Courtesy Archivo Magón.

As spring arrived, *Regeneración* became bolder. On March 23, the lead essay called "*Los Candidatos de la Dictadura*" (The Candidates of the Dictatorship) was a scathing three-and-a-half page (of a 16-page total paper) denunciation of the policies of Díaz. Reports of political discontent in Sonora followed, capped with an essay on the liberation of women, who were, according to the author or authors, "traditionally, seemingly content to be the frail victim of hypocrisy." The publication also pushed the limits with a long series called "*La Seguridad en la Republica*" which often began with a quote from Díaz and then countered with reports of banditry and malfeasance from all over Mexico.

The following edition, March 31 blasted Congress, but would not name deputies because "they serve the President, not the country (For this reason, we consider it immoral to name them)."

On April 7, *Regeneración* happily reported the resolution of the case against *El Hijo de Ahuizote*. Remigio Mateos, the director, was released after one year and two months in prison. A young man, Alfonso Cabrera (a relative of publisher Daniel Cabrera) had served seven months. The regime decommissioned Daniel Cabrera's printing equipment while returning D. Luis Mata's.

In the next edition, dated April 14, a long article on the presidency appeared, and in the middle of it was the line, "There is nothing more absurd than to call us revolutionaries... We are not revolutionaries because we want an end to the dictatorship...."

This was a foreshadowing of things to come: on April 23, a small item headlined "*Regeneración* has not died" was printed to squelch rumors officials spread in Northern Mexico that the paper was no more.

On May 15, 1901, *Regeneración* led with a rundown of all the "liberal clubs" in Mexico, and reported that when these clubs got together the first order of business was to pass several resolutions, the first of which was "to respect all laws."

It became obvious that Díaz had had enough. A week after the conference, both Jesús and Ricardo Flores Magón were sentenced to 12 months in Belen. According to historian Lomnitz, Enrique took over the editing chores, while Jesús and Ricardo smuggled their writings to him. The first issue Enrique was fully responsible for appeared on May 23. The lead article described the desperate situation of workers in Yucatan. On the last page of that issue, in large type, was the announcement that the brothers Jesús and Ricardo had been incarcerated. The masthead did not change in the next issue (May 31, 1901), but the lead story, "The persecution of the Press," did not mention the incarcerated Flores Magón brothers. Instead it named Díaz multiple times.

Enrique, a trained accountant, did not have either of his brothers' experience in publishing, and the paper reflected that. Notably, the headline writing was different, indicative of a person hand-setting the type and trying to make it fit by changing font sizes randomly within the headline itself. In the next issue, (June 7) there was a personal note from Jesús, transferring his legal clients to another lawyer, and the articles became longer. On June 15, 1901, Enrique reprinted an article from *El Hijo De Ahuizote* headlined "Persecution of *Regeneración*." It reported that the government had closed Filomeno Mata's shop. Then it went on to re-publish items from papers all over the country reporting the same event.

Yet another event hit the Flores Magón brothers hard that summer. In June, their mother, Margarita Magón died. Despite pleas to their jailers, the government allowed neither Jesús nor Ricardo to attend the funeral. In the following issue, Enrique ran a short item, apologizing for the late delivery of the paper to its subscribers. That, too, was blamed on Díaz.

Although the names of both Jesús and Ricardo remained on the masthead of *Regeneración*, neither would ever work within the confines of the offices of the paper again. When they were released in May 1902, Jesús bid good bye to the movement (he later served in the first revolutionary Madero cabinet). Enrique and Ricardo leased *El Hijo de Ahuizote* from the aging publisher Daniel Cabrera, himself serving time in Belen. The two brothers quickly joined him in Belen before Cabrera was released. Díaz had extended the old man's prison term for leasing his publication to the Flores Magón brothers. Undaunted, they managed to publish eight editions before being incarcerated. They were also instrumental in the formation of Mexico City's chapter of the Club Liberal.[66]

In Mexico, aside from the liberal clubs, 1902 was a time of silence for the opposition. Historians now recognize that the first five years of the 20th century cast a foreboding shadow on the nation's future. Due to self-interest, the *Porfirian* administration had left the country socially stunted, economically constricted and politically exclusive. Both the Mexican and international press kept the realities of Mexico from their readers, either through ignorance or by design. Mexico reached its economic breaking point in 1900, but this was not recognized at the time. According to many US papers, Porfirio Díaz was *the* statesman of his time. Seemingly single handedly, he transformed Mexico from a revolution-prone, economically backward country to a nation known to provide both preference and generous guarantees to foreign investors. The economic stability of Mexico was an illusion. The 1901 Pan-American Conference held in the capital became a media event. Diplomats from every sovereign nation in the western hemisphere except Chile attended the summit. The financial powers of the world believed the *Porfirian* magic could be duplicated in other parts of Latin America.[67]

The conference began in Mexico City in the spring and dragged on into November. The delegates failed to accomplish their goal of establishing a system of arbitration for international disputes in the Western Hemisphere. Still, reporters from all over the world, especially the United States, flocked to Mexico and international coverage of Mexican affairs was more common than at any time since the short reign of Maximilian. The number of articles increased dramatically from 1900 to 1901 – In 1901 the *New York Times* ran only ten stories about Mexico, but 42 the

---

[66] Cockcroft, James D., *Intellectual Precursors of the Mexican Revolution*, p. 98.
[67] *New York Times*, various issues, 1901; Roeder, pp. 100-105.

following year. The articles typically featured one of two Mexican attractions: business or the colorful president.[68]

Just as *Regeneración* was becoming more radicalized, the international press painted a glowing picture of the profits to be made from investments in Mexico and of the president who made those profits possible. "President Díaz," the *New York Times* boasted, "has succeeded in making himself not only loved by the common people but by the so-called aristocracy of the republic."[69]

The moneyed classes may or may not have loved Don Porfirio but they at least needed him. The poor classes were lucky to be ignored, since attention often meant brutality, deprivation of land or involuntary servitude in the Valle Nacional in southern Mexico. Papers simply did not report those social conditions – not in the foreign press and definitely not in the subsidized press of Mexico, which included all papers in Mexico City except *Regeneración* and *El Hijo de Ahuizote*. The foreign press reflected the imperialistic, exploitative mentality of the time. In a professional mining journal, an American mining engineer marveled at the capabilities of the Mexican miners who were paid about 25 cents (US) a day. He described them as looking like "undersized boys" who existed on a diet of corn and beans. "To see a group of four load a motor weighing 470 pounds on the back of a fifth gives one a curious sensation."[70]

Anglo prejudice relegated most Mexicans, especially those of color, to sub-human status and their plight was therefore ignored in the US press. For a Mexican publisher to report on the atrocities of the Díaz regime was, at the very least, economic suicide or garnered a sure-fire ticket to Belen

---

[68] *New York Times*, July 16, 1901; Index to the *New York Times*, 1860-1910.
[69] Ibid.
[70] Lamb, Mark R, "Mining labor and supplies in Mexico," *Engineering and Mining Journal*, December 26, 1908.

hospitality. Even the most radical of the anti-administration press presented abstract arguments concerning law rather than unfiltered descriptions of the real problems of Mexico. Hence, the reasoning of publishing *Regeneración* initially as a legal journal. But there was another factor that motivated the Mexican press apart from the fear of Belen: Many if not most of the Mexican inteligencia believed the country would flounder without Díaz.

When Ricardo Flores Magón described the Díaz administration as a "den of thieves" to the organizing members of the *Club Liberal* in 1901, he received hisses and boos. Two years later, it was a different story.[71]

In the summer of 1903, the *Club Liberal* published its manifesto, and convened its second convention in San Luis Potosi. The gap between the radicalism of the Flores Magón brothers and the club members had narrowed considerably as conservative members withdrew their support. The manifesto appeared in *Diario Del Hogar* in its entirety and "urged the resurrection of the institutions established by our fathers... to place limits on both church and state... we do not call you to revolution, but to save our country and to begin the measures necessary for our salvation. To this end, we are asking for the formation of many clubs, and with a sharp pen, to give a brief history of our country."[72]

That sharp pen, which called for a return to "order, the sanctity of law and guarantees of liberty," may well have been that of Ricardo Flores Magón. His style of writing was notable in that he addressed his audience directly, as did the manifesto. "Is there equality in our country? No. Does business prosper in our country? No. And so on, through a list of grievances that included the plight of agriculture, the

---

[71] Cockcroft, *Intellectual Precursors of the Mexican Revolution*, p. 98.
[72] Manifestación del Club Liberal *Ponciano Arriaga*, February 27, 1903, reprinted in Texto de Su Historia, pp. 301-302; the document is also republished in its entirety in Roeder, Volume II, pp. 208-909.

lack of educational opportunities, the lack of intellectual freedom, and the lack of respect for human life.[73]

The revolution was coming, Ricardo Flores Magón was sure of that. He also believed that he would be a major part of it for reasons he might never have fully comprehended. Revolutions, Roger D. Hansen wrote, are viewed from the standpoint of seemingly insignificant precipitating events, and pre-conditions or fundamental causes. Hansen noted that the revolution that was coming basically consisted of two distinct revolutions, and the Flores Magón brothers influenced both. The first revolution was the revolt of Indian Mexico, centered in Morelos, but extending to the neighboring states of Puebla, Guerrero, Mexico, and Hidalgo. Emiliano Zapata became the famous no-compromise leader of the Indian populations, and took as his slogan "Tierra y Libertad," straight from the masthead of editions of *Regeneración* published in the United States. Under the Díaz administration, the assault on the Indians of Mexico, both in terms of land expropriation and penal servitude had soared. The Flores Magón brothers were the only ones who had covered that situation.[74]

The second revolution, according to Hansen, was the *Mestizo* revolt, and looked "upward." Social and economic mobility had been closed to all but the *amigos* of Díaz, and these were the people who populated the liberal clubs. They were not concerned with the plight of the Indian population. The Flores Magón brothers were part of the initial movement, and the ties to this population were strengthened when Enrique used *Regeneración* as a kind of PLM national newsletter. Ricardo and Enrique built on these ties and bent them to their will in both Mexico and in the United States.[75]

---

[73] Ibid.
[74] Hansen, p. 152.
[75] Ibid, p. 153.

The Díaz regime outlawed the *Club Liberal* and arrested the most visible organizers. Yet, *Diario del Hogar* once again carried the slogan "No reelección" on its masthead, the slogan that brought Díaz to power some thirty years earlier. The paper covered the convention and the arrests that followed. Both Enrique and Ricardo Flores Magón arrived back in Belen. Ricardo and Juan Sarabía called for an investigation of the treatment of prisoners there and *El País* editorialized, "It is not the bastille!" This started an editorial war with Filomeno Mata, who replied that the prison he knew so well should be investigated. If Article 7 of the 1857 constitution were to be invoked, there would be no need for the prison.[76]

Earlier, Mata had complained about *El Imparcial* that while some journalists languished in prison, "friends of the government" published not only slander, but falsehoods. The worst, in Mata's eyes, was the *Mexico City Herald*, an English language daily, which he claimed provided the world with completely false information disguised as inept translation. In 1903, *El Diario* reported a quote of José Limantour in *El Imparcial* which said, "the plan does not contemplate placing Mexico on the gold standard immediately." The *Herald's* translation, "Mexico will abandon the silver standard and adopt the gold" potentially had serious consequences since the *Associated Press* also used this copy. There was, at the time, tremendous international pressure on Mexico to adopt the gold standard, but the measure would further separate the rich from the poor as Mexico was the largest silver producer in the world. Mata's beef with the Spanish language newspapers of Mexico City was different. They, he charged, had given into the "politics of silence."[77]

The Flores Magón brothers were silent. On April 2, Ricardo and Enrique faced arrest at a demonstration, carrying signs

---

[76] *Diario Del Hogar*, June 17, 1903 and July 1, 1903.
[77] Ibid, January 9 and May 19, 1903.

reading "*no reelección*" and on April 16, police raided the offices of *El Hijo de Ahuizote* once more. This time, Ricardo and Enrique went to jail for "ridiculing public officials" and held incommunicado for 34 days, then sent to Belen. They would not be released until October. It did not matter, since on July 9, the Supreme Court of Mexico banned the publication of anything written by the Flores Magón brothers. Their careers as Mexican journalists were over, but also just beginning.[78]

---

[78] Verter, pp. 343-344.

Chapter 5

Journalism, a Dangerous Game

When Ricardo and Enrique Flores Magón, as well as Santiago de la Hoz crossed into Texas on January 4, 1904, they were all famous – in Mexico. In Texas, they were unknown and almost penniless. All three took jobs as laborers in Laredo, Texas, but de la Hoz drowned two months later, on March 22, while swimming in the Rio Grande. The Flores Magón brothers did not believe it was an accident, and for good reason. If they were unknown in the United States, their work on *El Hijo de Ahuizote*, and Ricardo's work on the original *Regeneración* was well known in Mexico and certainly made them targets for the Díaz regime. Thomas Furlong, the man who arrested Ricardo in 1907, wrote in 1912 that he had tracked him for four years on orders of the Díaz government.[79]

The Flores Magón brothers had made their plans to relocate *Regeneración* to the United States during their last stint in Belen so they could continue writing anti-Díaz material without the risk of incarceration and death.

The suspicious drowning of their friend demonstrated that Texas, which had a separate extradition treaty with Mexico, might be offering a false sense of security. They continued with their plans nonetheless, in part because Jesús, who had left "the cause" but remained supportive of his brothers.

---

[79] Bufe, Verter, *Dreams of Freedom,* p. 344; Furlong, Thomas, *Fifty Years a Detective* (St. Louis: C. E. Barnett, 1912).

He had brought them money to buy food while they were doing their time in Belen. He also advised them, as later correspondence demonstrated, that he believed they could bring a case before US courts that would force Mexico to allow *Regeneración* to circulate through the Mexican mail system.

This case never materialized. Instead, prior to launching the re-born *Regeneración,* the brothers established a network of shopkeepers, many along the Texas-Mexico border, who smuggled the papers into Mexico. About one third of the contacts were in the United States, the rest in Mexico, especially the northern states of Coahuila, Chihuahua, Durango, and Sonora. The papers were hand-delivered at considerable risk. Under Díaz and his administration *Rurales* were known to shoot people simply for possessing a copy of *Regeneración* when it re-emerged. The Furlong agency obtained a subscription list when they raided one of the border distributors – it contained 693 names and addresses of Mexican subscribers.[80]

While circulation was a major problem, the more difficult challenge came from raising enough money. A man named Camilo Arriaga had paid for the flight from Mexico. He, too, was a fugitive and influenced Ricardo's political thinking early on. A member of a well-to-do mining family, he was well-connected in Mexico, even though he had also gone into exile in the United States. He continued to support *Regeneración* when it was published in San Antonio and arranged a $2,000 loan from none other than Francisco Madero to pay for the printing of the paper.[81]

---

[80] Roeder, *Hacia el México Moderno, Volumen II,* pp. 222-223; Turner, Ethel Duffy, *Revolution in Baja: Ricardo Flores Magón's High Noon* (Detroit: Blaine Ethridge Books, 1981), p. 69; Jesús to Ricardo, March 15, 1905, folder 2 of 14, Terrazas collection; Subscription listed Folder II A of 14, Terrazas Collection.
[81] Cockcroft, *Intellectual Precursors of the Mexican Revolution*, pp. 123-124.

The Flores Magón brothers had no intention of publishing a newspaper aimed at Mexican immigrants, and in one of the first issues, Enrique wrote what could never have been published in Mexico:

> Forever – for as long as Mexico can remember – today's slavery will be identified with the name of the devil who made it all possible. His name is Porfirio Díaz, and his bestiality is being carried out in Mexico... the *Jefes Politicos* do not send thieves and other criminals to jail – rather they sell them as slaves... you may say that Díaz does not benefit directly from this human commerce... but what about the governors of Veracruz, Oaxaca, Hidalgo, and other states, and their cronies who do benefit? ... The day of liberation is coming. Prepare yourselves, my fellow citizens.[82]

The brothers hoped to use their contacts in the *Clubes Liberales* to spread the call for armed revolution, and planned to send 30,000 copies of their paper into Mexico. This created a third, distinct element to the Mexican Press: Next to the official, heavily subsidized newspapers which preached *Continuismo*, and the moderately subsidized press, which called adherence to the constitution of 1857, now there were the Flores Magón brothers.[83]

Their beginning in the United States was not so auspicious. The first edition published in San Antonio appeared November 5, 1904. The paper was a four-page broadsheet, as *Regeneración* would remain from then on. It carried only two advertisements, one asking businesses to advertise in the publication, with the claim that it was being circulated in

---

[82] Meyer, Michael C. and Sherman, William L., *The Course of Mexican History* (Lincoln: University of Nebraska Press, 1967), pp. 485-486; The article is also reprinted in its entirety in Roeder, *Volume II*, pp. 235-237. Roeder credited the article to Enrique because Enrique had saved a copy.
[83] Turner, p. 60.

the southern United States and Mexico, and several notices calling for agents, both in the United States and Mexico.[84]

Ricardo Flores Magón's house in San Antonio on Cadalwater Street. Photo courtesy of Joseph R. Danel.

The November 5 edition listed Ricardo as Publisher, (*Director*), Enrique as Editor (*Administrator*) and Juan Sarabía as the lead writer/composer (*jefe de redacción*). For at least the fourth time, the lead article explained the purpose of the publication. "We return to combat, as we always have... To be precise: the tyranny of our country has become fearless." These words would become ironically prophetic, but the biggest concern at the moment was money. Enrique later claimed that the paper was running on the donations from Arriaga, the loan from Madero, and what

---

[84] *Regeneración*, November 5, 1904, accessed from *The Anarchist Annals of Ricardo Flores Magón* (http://archivomagon.net/periodicos/regeneracion-1900-1918/2da-epoca), accessed July 7, 2016.

he could contribute from his earnings as a worker outside the paper.[85]

Regeneración Editorial staff, San Antonio. Courtesy Archivo Magón.

Only 16 editions of *Regeneración* were published in San Antonio, and its distribution inside Mexico is hard to determine. But it did circulate freely throughout the Southwest, which, then as now, had a rather porous border with Mexico. The publication provided not only anti-Díaz propaganda but also topics that were not readily available in the Mexican or international press: The treatment of Indians, the influence of American corporations on the Mexican government and working conditions inside Mexico received coverage, sometimes for the first time. The publication attracted attention from both the Díaz government and the American left. The first was an immediate and ongoing problem, and the second would become a major detriment to Ricardo in later years.

Enrique Creel, then Governor of Chihuahua and soon to be Mexican ambassador to the United States, intercepted more than 3,000 letters with the help of the US government written

---

[85] Ibid, Roeder, Volume II, p. 233.

to the publication and its associates. Some of these letters contained subscription request, words of support and sometime even money. Creel kept a list of these supportive individuals and groups.[86] He also hired the Furlong Detective Agency, while Díaz or his minions sent gifts to officials in the United States government for their cooperation in the ongoing surveillance operation. The US Secret Service, operating under the code name "Joe Priest," kept the brothers and their associates under observation, as well.[87]

Meanwhile, *Regeneración* forged on for four months, publishing articles against the Díaz Regime. On November 12, an article characterized Ramon Corral, the vice president, "a major disappointment to the country." On an inside page, Díaz was blasted for his relationship with the Church. "General Díaz has not only murdered liberty, but he has killed the liberal spirit of the people. It is now impossible to be liberal." The article charged, that the Catholic Church was complicit, and Díaz, since his rise to power, had been a "good friend" to the Church.

General Bernardo Reyes, then still a Díaz favorite, was singled out for his action against newspapers. Perhaps to interest readership on the US side of the Rio Bravo, a long article decried the "depopulation of Mexico" because of immigration to the United States. The only advertisement in the paper was for a subscription -- $2 (US) in gold.[88]

The attacks against the Díaz regime continued, with articles on the *Cientificos*, violence against Mexican immigrants - supposedly perpetuated by Díaz - and an editorial calling for

---

[86] Flores Magón to Antonio Balboa, September 3, 1906, various letters, M-B, Folder 2 of 14, Terrazas Collection; Cockcroft, *Intellectual Precursors of the Mexican Revolution*, pp. 125-128.
[87] Cockcroft, *Intellectual Precursors of the Mexican Revolution*, p. 18.
[88] *Regeneración*, November 15, 1904, accessed from *The Anarchist Annals of Ricardo Flores Magón*,
(http://archivomagon.net/periodicos/regeneracion-1900-1918/2da-epoca), accessed July 7, 2016.

unity among Mexican liberals. By the fourth issue, the paper had attracted two advertisers: a local Spanish speaking doctor and a business college offering English-as-Second-Language classes.

Early on, several things became apparent: First, the newspaper had sources inside Mexico. Second, it was receiving and reprinting letters of praise from both sides of the border. Finally, while the newspaper continued to publish what news it could from the *Clubes Liberales* of Mexico (which were being prosecuted), it also published news of *Clubes Liberales* that were forming in the United States.[89]

The brothers had strong ties to the Mexican intellectual community, both in Mexico and to those who had fled. The people, who became associated with the publication in the next year, played important parts in both the upcoming revolution and the drafting of the 1917 constitution - people like Antonio Villarreal and Juan Sarabía's brother, Miguel. But it is safe to say that support from the working press of Mexico was lukewarm at best.

Silvestre Terrazas, the publisher of *El Correo de Chihuahua*, who knew of the Flores Magón brothers and at one time had even supported them. As *Regeneración* started anew in Texas, he reprinted an editorial from *La Opinión* in Veracruz, criticizing the Díaz regime and opposing the president's re-election. But the *El Grito del Puebla*, not *El Correo*, was the "radical" newspaper of Chihuahua, and neither paper editorially endorsed *Regeneración*, since that would be tantamount to calling for armed rebellion. When Don Silvestre drew fire from other newspapers in northern Mexico, he responded that his publication had only reprinted the editorial, not generated it. Reprinting controversial articles from other publications was a common ploy among

---

[89] Ibid, November 22, 1904, and December 3, 1904.

publishers who tried, as he did, to retain a level of political objectivity.[90]

Don Silvestre prospered in the publishing business and success made him an unlikely revolutionary until 1907. At mid-decade, *El Correo* boasted an adequate circulation (in one advertisement, he boasted of 2,000 subscribers) and enough advertising to expand and improve his facilities. The same year the Flores Magón brothers spent working as day labors in Texas, Don Silvestre imported the first linotype to Chihuahua and celebrated its installation by inviting local dignitaries, including Governor Creel, to a ceremony at the newspaper's office.[91]

Clearly, Don Silvestre viewed journalism as a business as well as a profession. The newspaper he had published in 1899 contained no advertising and no legitimate news – mistakes Don Silvestre would never make again. He was continually involved in improving the design and content of his paper, and actively solicited advertising sales. He reduced his column size in 1906 (which usually meant an increase in advertising revenues, even in a four-page paper) and increased staff.[92]

In later life, Don Silvestre wrote a book, *El Verdadero Pancho Villa*, in which he recounted his adventures as a civilian administrator for Villa. In later years, he tried to distance himself from Luis Terrazas as a "distant cousin," yet his daughter remembered going to the fiestas the Terrazas clan put on. Don Silvestre was a Johnny-come-lately to the anti-Díaz movement. Before the Revolution he had minor skirmishes with the government of Chihuahua, one over the famous Banco Minero robbery in 1908, and another over the accession of Enrique Creel, the alleged bank robber, to the governor's post. Creel was the son of a

---

[90] Personal Interview with Jane Dale Lloyd.
[91] Personal interview with Margarita Terrazas Perches in Ciudad de Chihuahua, June 30, 1986.
[92] Ibid.

US diplomat, who was born in Mexico and became the son-in-law of Don Luis Terrazas. Perhaps because of familial jealousies, an animosity developed between Creel and Don Silvestre.[93]

The situation in Chihuahua demonstrated a significant aspect of the *Porfiriato,* one which Don Silvestre was probably blithely unaware of, but the Flores Magón brothers understood simply because of their involvement with the original *Regeneración.* Díaz was thought to rule Mexico with an iron hand, but he did so through intermediaries, and each political Jefe dealt with different situations.

Chihuahua is often considered the birthplace of the Mexican Revolution. Far from Mexico City and economically tied to the United States, the *Chihuahuenses* recognized their unique problems early on and advocated states' rights as far back as the Mexican independence war. When asked what kind of government should rule Mexico in 1824, a Chihuahua delegate to the national congress said: "We are not interested in the problem. We want you to help us fight the Apache."[94]

Luis Terrazas ruled *Porfirian* Chihuahua. He owned more cattle than any individual in the world. A popular *Chihuahuense* story recalls the time when a US agent asked Don Luis if he could supply 70,000 head of cattle to feed US troops during the Spanish-American war. Don Luis replied, "What color?" The son of a butcher, Don Luis became rich because of the wars of the 1850s and 1860s. As a *Jefe Político*, he expropriated land for the government from the Church and landowners who supported the losing side. He

[93] Ibid, *Correo De Chihuahua*, June 30, 1906.
[94] Sandals, Robert Lynn, "Silvestre Terrazas, the Press and the origins of the Mexican Revolution," Doctoral Dissertation (Portland: Department of History, University of Oregon, 1967), p. 19.

then purchased the property himself or sold it at a discount to relatives.[95]

Díaz and Don Luis knew and distrusted each other for good reason. Don Luis became governor in Chihuahua in 1860. In 1871, he led *Chihuahuense* forces against Porfirian troops during Díaz 's revolt against Juarez. Díaz claimed victory in Chihuahua and placed one of his own men in the governor's chair. When Don Luis reclaimed the office after Díaz' electoral defeat in 1872, the unwritten peace accord between the two men supposedly included a verbal promise from Díaz never to set foot into Chihuahua again.

When Díaz became president in 1876 once again, he replaced Don Luis with his own appointee. However, the state legislature rejected that man and the famous landlord reclaimed the governorship in 1879. Expediently, he proclaimed himself a *Porfirista*. Thus began the uneasy truce between the president of Mexico and Don Luis Terrazas who not only controlled the cattle industry but had, or would have, monopolies in banking, beer and the iron works industry. He eventually owned the telephone and urban transit companies of Chihuahua, as well.[96]

Although the Flores Magón brothers and Don Silvestre were contemporaries, they were worlds apart. Don Silvestre returned from Mexico City to Chihuahua in 1894 after studying business administration and accounting. He must have known about the student protest in 1892 and the startup of *El Demócrata*. While he attended classes, Jesús sat in Belen. When Colonel Teodore Flores died in 1892, his family fell on hard times.

Essentially, Don Silvestre was part of the landed gentry of Chihuahua, and came home to a family, however "distant"

---

[95] Machado, Manuel, Jr., *The North Mexican Cattle Industry, 1910-1975: Ideology, Conflict, and Change* (College Station: Texas A&M University Press, 1981), pp. 4-5.
[96] Sandals, "Silvestre Terrazas, the Press and the origins of the Mexican Revolution," pp. 22-23.

from Don Luis, who still owned property. He immediately went to work as the personal secretary for Bishop Jesús Ortiz. Three people raised Don Silvestre's status from a basically in-line, profit-oriented newspaper publisher to revolutionary hero: Francisco Bulnes (one of the leading *Cientifico* intellectuals of the *Porfiriato*) called him "the intellectual author of the revolution in Chihuahua," Don Luis Terrazas considered him more important than Ricardo Flores Magón, and then there was Don Silvestre himself.[97]

Don Silvestre's social background made possible his employment with the church, which allied itself with the landed gentry. While he was not as wealthy as his grandparents' first cousin, Don Luis, he inherited a considerable amount of property from his parents as well as two estates from aunts. He enjoyed a reputation as a liberal thinker in Chihuahua, but his home life reflected the chauvinism of his time. He did not allow his children to play with the poor children of Chihuahua and he was adamantly opposed to any member of his family marrying anyone who even had a trace of Indian blood. His first public office was president of the Bicycle Club of Chihuahua.[98]

Under the direction of the always-politically active Bishop Ortiz, Don Silvestre was named editor of the *Revista Católica*. The weekly followed the church line: Liberalism foolishly freed men from restraints on their behavior, thereby creating secular evil that tore at the fabric of society. As a Catholic and a journalist who identified himself with the "Catholic Press," and had some misgivings about "positivism," the guiding philosophy of the *Cientificos*. Don Silvestre was influential in founding the Catholic Press

[97] Katz, Friedrich and Lloyd, Jane Dale, *Porfirio Díaz frente al descontento Popular Regional, 1891-1893* (México: Universidad Iberoamericana, 1986); Perches, Margarita Terrazas, "Biografía de Silvestre Terrazas, as published in Terrazas, Silvestre, *El Verdadero Pancho Villa* (Chihuahua: Talleres Gráficos del Gobierno de Estado de Chihuahua, 1984), p. 232; personal interview with Margarita Terrazas Perches, June 30, 1986.
[98] Ibid

Association of Mexico and later the Associated Press of the Mexican States, but he always dealt with the realities of relying on his allegiance to the Church and being a vassal of Don Luis.[99]

Don Silvestre combined the Church newspaper with a poetry magazine and launched *El Correo de Chihuahua* in 1899. He was, by all rights, a successful publisher and promised his advertisers a circulation of 2,000. His future, for the moment, was secure.

Not so for the Flores Magón brothers. In December 1904, in San Antonio, an intruder entered the home of Ricardo and tried to stab him in the back. The quick action of Enrique, who leaped on the man and subdued him, saved the brother. When the police arrived, they arrested Enrique for "disturbing the peace" and freed the assailant. Texas was not a safe haven.[100]

Their older brother agreed with them. Jesús had been instrumental in founding both *El Demócrata* in 1892, and *Regeneración* in 1900. He had meanwhile left the movement, and mildly opposed his brothers' fight against the regime. While morally and financially supportive of his brothers, Jesús did not believe the people of Mexico would support a violent revolution. He also feared for his brothers' safety. As a lawyer, he witnessed the corruption of the *Porfirian* courts on many occasions and knew that in Mexico protection under the law was a façade.[101]

He assessed the situation correctly. While in still in Mexico, Ricardo had found it necessary to protect himself from *Porfirian* thugs. He idealistically believed that he and his companions would find a haven in the United States, but he was wrong. After a short time in San Antonio, the brothers

---

[99] Sandals, p. 67; Zea, Leopoldo, *Positivism in Mexico*, translated by Josephine H. Schule (Austin: University of Texas Press, 1974), p.15.
[100] Bufe, Verter, p. 344.
[101] Jesús Flores Magón to Ricardo Flores Magón, June 7, 1904, M-B 18 part I, Folder Two of 14, Terrazas Collection.

decided to move their operation to St. Louis, thinking it would be safe to publish a paper in what Ethel Duffy Turner described as "the heart of a nation that guaranteed freedom of the press." Jesús agreed that the move to St. Louis was prudent. "I am glad you are leaving San Antonio," he wrote to Ricardo. "I'm sure that Saint Louis will be better and you will be able to work with more freedom." He also advised Ricardo to consult with government authorities in Missouri and study US laws concerning extradition.[102]

Incredibly, *Regeneración* relocated to St. Louis in February 1905 without missing an edition. Relocating any newspaper office across town – even today – is a gargantuan task. Moving a hand-set weekly, even if it only contained four pages, is an incredible feat, and one that went unnoticed by the historians who have written about the newspaper and the Flores Magóns. A weekly newspaper survives on dependability, and that means it has to come out every week. This was not even a "local" weekly. Readers spread throughout the American Southwest and Mexico. In the first paper appearing in St. Louis on February 25, a front-page article explained "one more time, we are obliged to change our residence to seek safety to make our political work possible." This appeared under the headline, "the relentless persecution of the dictatorship," and explained "deprivations of General Díaz know no boundaries." The staff had managed to sign up three advertisers, all from San Antonio: One from a news and advertising service that dealt with Mexico, a second from an agency selling tickets in Spanish, ironically, for parties celebrating the birthday of George Washington, both in San Antonio and Laredo, and a third from a hairdresser.[103]

---

[102] Jesús Flores Magón to Ricardo Flores Magón, March 15, 1905. M-B 18 Part I, folder2 of 14; Cockcroft, pp. 123-124.
[103] *Regeneración*, February 25, 1905, accessed from *The Anarchist Annals of Ricardo Flores Magón*
(http://archivomagon.net/periodicos/regeneracion-1900-1918/2da-epoca) accessed July, 2016. Translation by author.

If there was trouble behind, there was trouble ahead, but the Flores Magón brothers could not tell where it was coming from, and it would arrive for all directions of the political scale.

The following is taken from a transcript published from the archives of *El Partido Liberal Mexicano*. It was printed in Spanish, and the interview probably took place in Spanish.

Detective: Do you know the staff of *Regeneración*?

Informant: Yes, I know them very well, since you commissioned me four months ago.

D: What are their names?

I: They are called Ricardo Flores Magón, Enrique Flores Magón, Juan Sarabía, Antonio I. Villarreal and Rosalío Bustamante.

D: Can you give me a description of these men.

I: Yes sir, it follows:

Ricardo Flores Magón, five foot, 8 inches tall, heavy set, about 28 years old. His hair and eyes are black. He is olive-skinned.

D: Does he smoke?

I: He is a great smoker of *cigarros*.

D: Does he talk much?

I: He is a very serious, but he has the ability to talk and express himself elegantly.

D: Does he speak English?

I: Very little.

D: Is he straight forward?

I: Enough.

D. Is he married?

I: No.

D: What else can you tell me about Señor Magón?

I: He is a very intelligent newspaper man, a worker, active, he never gets drunk and he is a good typist. He has respect for his companions and is a fanatic for the cause he pursues, he is brutally fanatic and dangerous because of the anarchists.[104]

And the informant went on to describe all of them in a likewise manner. Enrique, he said, seemed "more American" but did not have his brother's intellect. Juan Sarabía was a man of good humor, but not as important as Ricardo Flores Magón. Antonio Villarreal had the real confidence of Ricardo Flores Magón. He was the one responsible for collecting the money, and he was as fanatical as Ricardo.

The detective wanted to know more specifics. Did the group have any connections with the Mexican consul in St. Louis? No. That was logical since they had first established their newspaper on the border, then moved it to St. Louis, the informant said. It was liked very much by some Mexican people because it was "against the government and the rich" and these circumstances helped augment the circulation of *Regeneración*. He also identified the editors of *El Colmillo Publico* as "friends of Flores Magón." [105]

The detective wanted to know if the informant felt that Flores Magón was a threat to the United States. The informant did not think so, as he had expressed admiration for the US

[104] "Información secreta que el agente N.N., de Saint Louis, Missouri, le dio al suscrito [Enrique Creel], contestando el siguiente interrogatorio" (October 28, 1906), reprinted in *El Partido Liberal Mexicano, 1906-1908* (México: Ediciones Antorcha, 1986), pp. 262-272, Translation by Author.
[105] Ibid.

government in terms of freedom of the press. But then the interview got more pointed:

D. Do you know if they bought arms?

I: I do not know.

D: Do you know if they bought dynamite or other explosives?

I: I do not know.

D: What states in Mexico received the publication?

I: Sonara, Coahuila, Nuevo León, San Luis Potosí and Veracruz.

D. Do you know Librado Rivera?

I: I don't know him very well, he is a man of little importance…

D: Do you know if the Magóns have relationships with any Mexican officials?

I: I don't know, but I believe not, because they haven't had correspondence with any. Sometimes there were heated discussions about General Bernardo D. Reyes, but these conversations about politics and people were not in my presence.

But then he added: You already know that during the four months I worked with them, there was information and articles about General Díaz, Señor Corral, General Terrazas, Señor Creel and other people... but I never knew the names of the correspondents...

D: Of the total *Regeneración* group, who do you consider the most dangerous.

I: Without a doubt, Ricardo Flores Magón.

D: Do you believe they are capable of creating a revolutionary movement?

I: Yes, sir, I believe that completely.

D: And if Ricardo Flores Magón was apprehended and placed in prison for a number of years, could they succeed?

I: That act would end the movement, because he, Don Ricardo, is the soul of the movement and without him, nothing would happen. I will repeat that; it would end it completely.[106]

Safety had been a major concern when *Regeneración* relocated to St. Louis. As noted, Texas had an individual extradition treaty with Mexico, and libel cases in Mexico were both civil and criminal, and in the hands of an appointed judge. The paper still relied on contributions and subscriptions, but the subscription list had grown to more than 20,000, compared to 2,000 for *El Correo de Chihuahua*, and those subscribers spread throughout Mexico and the southwestern states of the United States.

While the subscriptions sold for 3.5 pesos in Mexico, both the Mexican and US governments confiscated much of this money. The brothers could only pay themselves a salary of $10 a week or less. Jesús had been sending his brothers what money he could, but by September 1905, he was becoming even more disenchanted with the idea of revolution. He wrote them: "Although you call me an alarmist, and many other things that you may think but do not tell me... I will repeat a thousand times that the road of revolution is the one I will follow the least." Later in the month, he reiterated his concerns: "I don't believe the people are ready for a revolution, and I also do not believe you have enough prestige to provoke a fight."[107]

---

[106] Ibid.

[107] Turner, Ethel Duffy, p. 75; 15-page subscription list dated 1906, M-B 18, part I, folder 11A of 14, Terrazas Collection; Jesús Flores Magón to Ricardo Flores Magón, September 19 and September 27, 1905, M-b 18 part I, folder 2 of 14, Terrazas Collection.

Through the summer of 1905, the paper still had the support of Camilo Arriaga, at least in the form of a standing advertisement for his export company, but that was about to change. Throughout its US tenure, *Regeneración* had continued to publish broadsides against Díaz and his administration. It continually published articles on the debt peonage in Mexico, working conditions and mistreatment of Mexican Indians. Undoubtedly, they had solid connections with the intelligentsia of Mexico who provided them with the information to enable them to write these stories.

These connections developed during the rise of the *Clubes Liberales* in Mexico. That group was basically anti-clerical and anti-re-electionist. At the same time, the unknown informant spilled his guts to an unnamed investigator, Ricardo Flores Magón took steps that would distance him from these supporters. While in the United States, *Regeneración* had published multiple articles, calling for the reformation of the *Clubes Liberales*, both in Mexico and among Mexicans in the United States who had come over to work. On September 28, 1905, the newspaper crossed a line: It published the manifesto of the *Partido Liberal Mexicano* (on page 2, probably to avoid censorship at the post office), the PLM, and announced as president Ricardo Flores Magón, Juan Sarabía as vice president, Antonio Villarreal as secretary, and Enrique as Treasurer.[108]

Camilo Arriaga dropped them like a hot potato, and "the junta" was in jail less than two weeks later. Díaz sent an emissary to St. Louis to bring charges of criminal libel against them. The Pinkertons raided the St. Louis office of *Regeneración.* All the equipment was confiscated and sold. The Flores Magóns stayed in jail until December, when they were bailed out. Most of the money came from American leftists. Verter estimated that by the time the brothers were

---

[108] *Regeneración*, various editions, summer of 1905 and September 30, accessed from *The Anarchist Annals of Ricardo Flores Magón* (http://archivomagon.net/periodicos/regeneracion-1900-1918/2da-epoca), accessed July 9, 2016.

arrested, the circulation of *Regeneración* had exceeded 20,000, maybe reached as much as 30,000. Because of the clandestine nature of the delivery system, there is no way of knowing an exact number.

Juan Sarabía mug shot. Courtesy http://revistabicentenario.com.mx/.

Arriaga distanced himself from them simply because of the growing ties between the Flores Magón brothers and the American left wing, particularly the International Workers of the World. Although Ricardo and Enrique Flores Magón had not yet begun to disseminate material considered radical in terms of anarchic-syndicalism, the takeover of the *Clubes Liberales* movement obviously did not sit well with Mexicans who continued to oppose the administration in Mexico. Without actually calling for an anarchist state, the brothers had inadvertently opened the question of what, exactly, was a "liberal." This created controversy on both sides of the border. In Mexico, the movement was both anti-clerical and anti-Díaz, but the stripes were broader on the American left:

Was a liberal a communist? A socialist? An Anarchist? A reformer?[109]

---

[109] Bufe, Verter, p. 345; for a discussion of the differences on the left, see Lomnitz, pp. 232-235.

Chapter 6

"A Man named Magoon"

Northern Mexico provided a natural setting for revolution. In a sense, the area was to Mexico what the American "West" was to the United States: a distant land populated by pioneers who cherished their independence from the federal government. The foreign commercial interests characterized its economy. It was also populated by indigenous people who resented the intrusion of the "pioneers."

Mining and railroads brought fledgling unions to the "hot country." In Douglas, Arizona, a newly-formed Western Federation of Miners chapter would play a part in the troubles coming to a place called Cananea. Mexican miners who toiled there were among the highest-paid laborers in Mexico, but they were also aware of how poorly their wages compared to those of their counter-parts in the United States and particularly to those US citizens employed in the Cananea mines at the time. The Mexican miners were paid about half.

The strike lasted less than 36 hours, and was crushed when mine owner William Greene brought 200 strikebreakers and Arizona rangers to the scene. The resulting violence left almost two dozen striking miners dead and got a lot of press, both in Mexico and the United States. For the first time, the US public became aware of the possibility of a Mexican Revolution, and the abundance of anti-US sentiment in Mexico.

Although the strike received massive coverage in both countries, the emphasis was much different. Silvestre Terrazas devoted considerable space in his paper *El Correo de Chihuahua* . The coverage began four days after the strike (a typical delay in coverage in Mexican news at the time), and included photographs of the US "volunteers" in Cananea. Don Silvestre ran an accurate front page news story on the strike that ended by accusing the Díaz government of collaborating with US economic interests against Mexico. On June 8, the paper reprinted a critical article from *El Tiempo* in Mexico City that said, in part:

> It has been shown that the Americans were responsible, and that the (Mexican) multitude were disarmed and peaceful... This castigation (of the Americans) is necessary because it shows foreigners that that when they are in a different land, they should respect the law."[110]

The reaction in the United States was different. The US press, especially the Associated Press, spurred by both imagination and nationalistic fervor, quoted a near-hysterical telegram from a US consular official that read, in part, "all of our lives are in danger!" The US press treated the story as an indication of the rising tide of anti-Americanism in Mexico and unwittingly displayed American prejudice against Mexicans. For the exaggerated AP story, the *Great Falls (Montana) Tribune* created this headline"

MURDERED IN MEXICO
Enraged Greaser slaughter
Forty-five Americans below Arizona Line
GREEN'S CAMP DOOMED
Drunken Mexican use dynamite to
Blow Up Great Mills and Smelters
In Prosperous Copper Camp

---

[110] *El Correo de Chihuahua*, June 4, 6 and 8, 1906.

Troops Sent to Capture and Punish Ringleaders.[111]

Only four Americans had been killed, while 18 Mexicans died in the violence. Subsequent Associated Press reports, as well as other sources, reported there were no dynamiters and little, if any, drinking by the Mexican strikers. *El Correo* published the major demand of the strikers: an end to the two-tier wage system for Mexican and US miners. Don Silvestre had his own editorial bias. While aware of the necessity of US investment in Mexico, *El Correo* indulged in the accepted practice of criticizing American activities and those of US citizens in Mexico.[112]

Don Silvestre and Governor Enrique Creel (soon to be named the Mexican ambassador to the United States) differed on their views of US interests in Mexico. Creel and his father-in-law controlled the power structure in Chihuahua, which benefited directly from doing business with the United States. Since 1898, Creel had served on the board of *El Banco Central Mexicano*, used heavily by the Mexican government. In Chihuahua, the Terrazas-Creel clan owned 80 percent of *Banco Minero* and held monopolies in many industries, including the Chihuahua phone company and trolley system. By the end of the *Porfiriato*, the family owed 7 million acres of land and more than 1.5 million cattle. The total (US) value of the clan was estimated at more than $25 million.[113]

Don Silvestre wrote for an audience he perceived to be exploited by the United States. He believed US investment was good for Mexico, but resented the attitudes of some US businessmen in Mexico. In August 2006, he criticized

---

[111] *New York Times*, June 2 and 3, 1906; *Great Falls Tribune*, June 3, 1906.

[112] *El Correo de Chihuahua*, June 4, 6 and 8, 1906.

[113] Alameda, Francisco R., *La Revolución en el Estado de Chihuahua, Tomo I* (Chihuahua: Biblioteca del Instituto Nacional de Estudios Históricos de la Revolución Mexicana, 1964).

William Greene, the man against whom the Mexican miners had struck:

> He is permitted the luxury of cruising the continent in sumptuous special cars; playing the stock market which allows him to stand with impunity, rifle in hand, pistol at his belt, before a mass of workers, who answer rifle shots with stones; for this [reason] he can employ 12,000 workers to whom he only pays a salary imposed by a well-known principle of political economy, that teaches us that prices of property, like salaries, are subject to supply and demand... It is false, foolish and stupid to assert that he pays double what other companies pay... in Cananea he pays mine laborers 3.50 pesos a day... in Santa Eulalia... where the cost of living is 30 to 40 percent less than in Cananea, they are paid 2.50 and 3.00 pesos.[114]

On both sides of the border, people were looking for somebody to blame for the strike in Cananea and its violent end, and that quickly. It wasn't hard. Creel had spent considerable time and money to track the St. Louis Junta. While both the Mexican and US government were aware of the Ricardo Flores Magón, neither the US press or public knew anything about him. When Mexican officials accused the junta of culpability for the strike, Greene was quick to join in. Both *the New York Times* and the Associated Press, in the articles on Greene's allegations, displayed their ignorance of the situation in Mexico and the personalities involved. The *Times* referred to him as a "man named Magoon," while the Associated Press called him "R. Flores Magood."

As much as Don Ricardo would have liked to have started the revolution there, he was in Canada at the time. He had been arrested in October, 1905 and had been in jail in St. Louis until December, along with Enrique and Juan Sarabía.

---

[114] *El Correo de Chihuahua*, August 24, as translated in Sandals, p. 108.

Supporters in Mexico but also members of the American left raised the bail money. *Regeneración* began publishing again on February 1, 1906, and in a front-page article, explained that once, again, they had been shut down because of persecution. The inside pages contained articles on the war against the Yaqui Indians in Sonora, several articles criticized the Díaz government, and Magón published two legalistic proclamations from the PLM. The next edition did not appear until February 15. The lead article predicted the end of *Porfirian* rule. The paper also included a report from the PLM club of Douglas, Arizona, and several proclamations from the PLM Junta.

The next issue also took two weeks, and contained fewer news from Mexico, but more proclamations from the Junta. The March 15 issue had a boxed front-page plea for advertising and financial support. By the time, it hit the streets, Ricardo, Enrique and Juan Sarabía were on their way to Canada, leaving the publication of *Regeneración* to Antonio I. Villarreal, Librado Rivera and Juan Sarabía's brother, Manuel. The masthead did not change, but it listed Villarreal as a secondary reporter.[115]

For the rest of his life, Ricardo would be in jail, in court, or on the run from detectives. His reasons for leaving St. Louis were threefold. First, he believed that a libel suit brought against him in a Mexican court by Mexican officials and businessman could result in his eventual extradition to Mexico. Second, he did not believe he could continue work on the PLM manifesto under the constant surveillance of detectives. Finally, he believed that Canada protected his and his associates' civil liberties from the Pinkertons and the

---

[115] *Regeneración*, February 1, February 15, March 1, March 15, March 30, 1906, accessed from *The Anarchist Annals of Ricardo Flores Magón* (http://archivomagon.net/periodicos/regeneracion-1900-1918/2da-epoca), accessed July 7, 2016.

Furlong Detective Agency. He was wrong. The Furlong Agency stayed on their heels.[116]

Two weeks after the strike, the PLM issued its proclamation calling for radical change in the Mexican government. The program contained 52 separate points, all in basic disagreement with the Porfiriato. These included clauses that prohibited the reelection of the president, curtail the power of military and political bosses, and guarantee freedom of the press. The program was a double-edged sword, because not only did it criticize the Díaz regime but it also called for strict limits on foreign involvement in the political and economic life of Mexico. It urged Mexicans to choose between liberty and "humiliation before foreigners." Supposedly, many PLM supporters worked on the program and it was not as radical as Ricardo would have liked. Still, it was the most radical document Mexican politics ever produced and surpassed the Constitution of 1917, which drew heavily on ideas of the PLM, especially with respect to labor and land reform.[117]

While the PLM program is revered in Mexican history, its publication in 1906 was detrimental to the PLM cause. Many well-to-do Mexican PLM supporters, beginning to feel the crunch of Mexico's facing economy and the world-wide economic recession of 1907-1910, withdrew their support. The Mexican press, official and independent alike, unanimously opposed radicalism and both Filomeno Mata in Mexico City and Silvestre Terrazas in Chihuahua, cut their ties with Flores Magón. He represented the threat of violent revolution, something unacceptable to all publishers in Mexico. These men continued to believe the future would be best served by simple enforcement of the constitution of 1857. PLM efforts were further damaged in September when Francisco Madero publicly rebutted the PLM. "Díaz is

[116] Bufe, Verter, p. 345.
[117] "Programa del Partido Liberal", Julio 1, 1906, as reprinted in *La Revolución Mexicana*, Tomo I; Cockcroft, p. 30.

not a tyrant," he told a reporter. "He may be somewhat rigid, but he is not a tyrant."[118]

Ricardo traveled from Canada to El Paso in August to organize an armed revolution against Díaz. The fortunes of the PLM were quickly waning. The junta could only afford transportation to Texas for two men. Enrique had to stay in Canada working as a day laborer for $9 a week, while Librado Rivera struggled to continue publishing *Regeneración* in St. Louis. A US Postal Service decision that all copies of the paper be sent by first-class mail hurt the publication in February.[119]

Librado Rivera and Enrique Flores Magón.
Courtesy Library of Congress, LC-B2- 2206-7 [P&P].

History, through the visage of time, can be viewed as tragedy or farce, and there were certainly elements of

---

[118] Personal interviews with Jane Dale Lloyd and Margarita Terrazas Perches; Cockcroft, p. 129.
[119] Turner, Ethel Duffy, *Revolution in Baja*, p. 94 and p. 103.

tragedy in the records of the PLM in 1907 and 1908. There was also material that George Bernard Shaw could have translated into one of his plays about over-zealous but under-powered military personalities. After Cananea, Ricardo Flores Magón thought of himself as a military man. In July, he sent a dispatch from Canada via the St. Louis Junta to his revolutionaries in Mexico and along the border, to be ready at his command.

For several years Ricardo must have been aware that in Mexico he had more supporters than guns. The archives of the PLM confirm that the revolutionary budget included $180 for three Winchester rifles, a .44 carbine, and $50 for a horse as expected expenditures. The PLM had more prospective officers than weapons. Another archival document lists 32 men for possible military positions, ranging from two generals to a director of music. The addresses on the list were exclusively in Texas.[120]

PLM supporters, operating from Texas and Arizona, claimed credit for several small skirmishes in Northern Mexico between 1906 and 1908, but the revolutionaries were easily defeated. In El Paso, US authorities arrested and jailed Antonio Villarreal for several months. In October 1906, Juan Sarabía and nine others were arrested in Mexico. Some of the men received fines and prison sentences from one month to two years. Those who were closely linked to Flores Magón were given long prison terms and shipped to Mexico City where they remained until Díaz resigned in 1911. Ricardo kept moving.

Don Ricardo later described that period to Ethel Duffy Turner: "The secret services of the two countries chased me from one place to another, from city to city. It was a question

---

[120] "Instrucciones generales a los revolucionarios," Julio, 1906, "S. Espinosa to Ricardo Flores Magón, Augusto 20, 1907," and "Propician de Nómbrelos", undated, unsigned, as published in *El Parido Liberal Mexicano (1906-1908)* (México: Ediciones Antorcha, 1986), pp. 66, 186, 136, respectively.

of life or death for me, because my arrest would mean my immediate passage to Mexico and murder without any appearance of justice."[121]

There were only 13 editions of *Regeneración* published in 1906, the last one on August 1. The paper had largely become a mouthpiece for the policies of the Junta, with all their members spending most of their time running and trying to avoid police and detectives. In Canada, Díaz had placed a $20,000 reward on Ricardo's head. He started moving through the United States, first to Texas, then to California, moving to San Francisco, then to Sacramento, and finally to Los Angeles, where he arrived in June of 1907. By then, 100,000 copies of wanted posters were being distributed in the United States, bearing a reward for $25,000 for his capture.[122]

Porfirio Díaz and Ricardo Flores Magón at last had something in common in 1907. Both were losing their grip on reality. Don Ricardo believed that the down-trodden of Mexico would rise to his call, even though his older brother had told him years before that Mexico was not ready for an armed revolution. Don Porfirio was 77 years old then, and had ruled Mexico for 36 years. He had created the very class system that would bring about his downfall. Early on in his presidency, there had been economic mobility for *mestizos*, and many of them found themselves moving up in Mexican society. That began to stall in the 1890s, when the *Cientificos* began their rise to power. The *Cientificos* were creoles or Europeans, and most of them had begun their careers as young and talented lawyers. They served as representatives of the foreign investors, arranged

---

[121] Alameda, tomo I, p. 114; Turner, p. 114.
[122] *Regeneración*, February 1, to August 1, 1906, accessed from *The Anarchist Annals of Ricardo Flores Magón* (http://archivomagon.net/periodicos/regeneracion-1900-1918/2da-epoca), accessed July 10, 2016; Bufe, Verter, pp. 345-348.

banking and industrial concessions, and expedited legal procedures.

By the end of the *Porfiriato* they held three cabinet positions, eight sub secretariats, twelve governorships, 25 senatorial seats, and half the seats in the Chamber of Deputies. These men believed that the leadership of Mexico must be white. They created a rift between themselves and the increasingly discontent *Mestizo cacique* group that turned toward General Bernardo Reyes for leadership. Díaz seemed blissfully unware of all of this, just as Ricardo Flores Magón was unaware of the lurking policemen who kicked in his door in Los Angeles in the late afternoon hours of August 23, 1907.[123]

---

[123] Hansen, pp. 154,155.

Chapter 7

"The American Problem"

n the annals of human conflict, there are few, if any, instances where writers played a more important part than in the lead up to the Mexican Revolution in the years between 1908 and 1910. It was a series of articles and books that led Mexico into the bloodiest civil war ever fought on the North American continent. Other than a few historians, no one remembers these works. When the revolution broke out, the man who may well have been Mexico's most gifted writer was locked up. Ricardo Flores Magón spent those years in California jails and Arizona prisons. The articles and books by James Creelman, Francisco Madero and John Kenneth Turner did not become literary "classics," but they certainly demonstrated the road to Hell is paved with good intentions.

The single most important contribution of US journalism to Mexican history is a 45-page article published by James Creelman, a Canadian, in the March 1908 edition of *Pearson's Magazine*. Many books on the Mexican Revolution begin with the Creelman interview of Porfirio Díaz. Unwittingly, the two men, reporters and subject, had opened the floodgates of revolution.

The laudatory article began:

From the heights of the Chapultepec Castle, President Díaz looked down upon the venerable capital of his country, spread out on a vast plain, with

87

a ring of mountains flung up grandly about it, and I, who had come nearly four thousand miles from New York to see the master and hero of Modern Mexico – the inscrutable leader in whose veins is blended primitive Mixtec with that of the invading Spaniards – watched the slender, erect form, the strong, soldierly head and commanding, but sensitive, countenance with an interest beyond words to express.[124]

The article continued in the same vein and on the second page, Creelman demonstrated the classic case of what journalists call the "buried lead" (inadvertently not putting the most important news in the first paragraph):

Yet today, in the supremacy of his career, this astonishing man – foremost figure of the American hemisphere and unreadable mystery to students of human government – announces that he will insist on retiring at the end of his present term, so that he may see his successor peacefully established and that, with his assistance, the people of Mexico may show the world they have entered serenely and preparedly upon the last complete phase of their liberties.[125]

The US press largely ignored the revelation. The news item did not even appear in the *New York Times*. Then, as now, many magazines were on the stands long before their official publication date, and the interview was reprinted first the *Mexican Herald*. *El Tiempo*, a pro-catholic newspaper, and *El Imparcial* published a translation on March 4.[126]

The pro-Díaz press in Mexico used the occasion of the president's retirement for a series of laudatory articles. The independent press, however, was more skeptical, since the

---

[124] Creelman, James "President Díaz, Hero of the Americas," *Pearson's Magazine*, March, 1908.
[125] Ibid.
[126] Guzmán, Diego Arenas, *Periodismo en la Revolución Mexicana*, (México: Biblioteca de Instituto Nacional de Estudios Históricos de la Revolución Mexicana, 1966), p. 4.

interview had been conducted by a *gringo* reporter. *Diario del Hogar* complained:

> In the few lines, we have copied, there are omissions that demonstrate the reporter forgot or never knew Mexican history... [he] wanted to pay elegant tribute to our president, but forgot to record the politicians who formed the base and won these rights for Mexico. It doesn't surprise us that the *Yankee* made these omissions, but it does surprise use that those newspapers who claim to be friends of the government did not report them.[127]

Many Mexican publishers, including Mata and Terrazas, did not believe that Díaz would retire. They pointed out that the article was intended for American readers. On March 18, *El Correo de Chihuahua* discredited the Creelman interview and quoted an anonymous source: "The president will respond to the mandate of the Mexican people." Chihuahua was far removed from Mexico City and Don Silvestre considered wishing his cousin Luis a happy birthday more important than debating election results that were determined elsewhere and had little or no effect on Chihuahua. Six months after the Creelman interview was published in Mexico City, *El Correo* reported, matter-of-factly, that Díaz had decided to accept another term because of the ongoing trouble with the Yaquis.[128]

Immediately after the interview appeared in Mexican newspapers, Díaz refused to comment to Mexican newspapers on his political plans, even to the pro- Díaz press. His intentions are a matter of speculation to this day, but the interview indicates that Díaz may have had an exaggerated estimation of his own popularity. The fact that a reporter from a US publication conducted the interview reflected Díaz's attitude toward the Mexican press. Around

---

[127] *Diario del Hogar*, April 15, 1908.
[128] *El Correo de Chihuahua*, March 2, 16, 18, 1908, June 22, 1908 and July 7, 1908.

the time when he sat down with James Creelman, he routinely refused requests for interviews from Mexican newspapermen.

However, not all Mexican journalists wanted to interview him. A growing contingent of labor-oriented publications found a ready market among Mexicans working in mining, railroad and industry. Media abhors a vacuum. This was a market *Regeneración* targeted to some extent until Ricardo Flores Magón fled to Canada in March 1906. That year marked a divide between Mexican labor and the St. Louis junta, as expressed in a song a textile worker wrote in Rio Blanco:

Y no somos anarquistas, ni queremos rebelión, [sino) menos horas de trabajo y buena distribución (We are not anarchist, and don't want a revolution [but] a shorter work day and a better deal.[129]

As long as the labor publications did not openly affiliate with the PLM, Díaz ignored the inexpensive papers that sprung up throughout the country, such *as El Diablo Bromista*, a "weekly for the working class, the whip for an evil *bourgeoisie*." After the St. Louis junta was incarcerated in a Los Angeles jail and the administration ended union strikes in Mexico by shooting several hundred workers in Rio Blanco, Veracruz, the Díaz administration became somewhat complacent to unionism.[130]

But support for unions increased throughout Mexico, reflecting a growing discontent among the populace. Those Mexicans who found employment in the mines, with the railroads and in the textile mills earned a better income than their fellow countrymen who worked in agriculture. Yet they

[129] As translated in Knight, Alan, *The Mexican Revolution, Volume I: Porfirians, Liberals and Peasants* (Lincoln, London: University of Nebraska Press,1986), p. 137. Knight observes that after 1906 there was "scant evidence" of PLM involvement in the Mexican Labor Movement.
[130] Cumberland, Charles Curtis, *The Mexican Revolution: Genesis under Madero* (New York: Greenwood Press, 1952), pp. 24 and 25.

still received much less than US citizens working in the same industries in Mexico. This discrepancy became a favorite topic for some Mexican journalists, including Silvestre Terrazas. "The American problem," as Don Silvestre called it, became another argument for political change in Mexico.[131]

Political change depended on the retirement of Díaz. In October 1908, Filomeno Mata published an open letter to Díaz, demanding that he confirm or deny the contents of the Creelman interview. Díaz replied that his statements were only expressions of "personal desire." The revelation, at least for Francisco Madero, came too late. After the Creelman interview, several writers published books calling for the formation of political parties and urging political responsibilities on the part of the masses. A wealthy landowner, Madero wrote the most important of these, *La sucesión presidencial en 1910 (The Presidential Succession of 1910)*. He arranged for its printing and was waiting only for the permission of his family to proceed.[132]

Madero was part of the landed gentry of Mexico, coming from a family that had massive estates in Coahuila and Nuevo Leon. Educated in the United States and France, the 35-year-old *hacendado* had been exposed to eastern mysticism while reading the *Bhagavad Gita* (Song of Heaven) of the Hindu faith. According to post-revolutionary mythology, Madero began his involvement in Mexican politics because of a "supernatural" experience he had concerning "spirit writing," after returning to the family hacienda in Coahuila.[133]

At any rate, Madero adopted the Hindu belief that "there is nothing better than a righteous battle." He became active in

---

[131] *El Correo de Chihuahua*, various editions in 1906-1908.
[132] *Diario del Hogar*, October 27.1910; Ross, Stanley, *Francisco Madero, Apostle of the Mexican Revolution* (New York: Columbia University Press, 1955), p. 36.
[133] Ibid, pp. 8 and 9.

the Coahuila gubernatorial election in 1904. The fledgling politician helped fund the political weekly *El Demócrata de San Pedro* and wrote several articles for it. His family did not look kindly upon his political ambitions. Madero's grandfather Evaristo, the family patriarch, wrote to him, warning him about fruitless opposition and comparing his endeavors to the regime to "the rivalry of a microbe and an elephant." Madero reassured his family that he intended only to pursue political ends within the law, and, as noted earlier, had withdrawn his support of the PLM at the first hint of armed revolt.[134]

Madero represented those Mexicans who wanted political opportunity and who could appreciate, because of their status and education, what political opportunity could mean for them. Conversely, Madero did not represent the majority of the Mexican people, who were chiefly concerned with getting enough food to stay alive. During the Porfiriato, approximately 27 percent of the total area of Mexico transferred from public to private ownership (for the total of some $12 million), and the Madero family, like the Terrazas family, were beneficiaries. Ninety percent of the population owned no land. Hacendados owned more than 50 percent of the Mexican land base, and Madero had no intention of advancing the cause of the landless masses.[135]

As a member of the economic elite of Mexico, Madero hoped only to break the political stranglehold the Cientificos had on the country, not to redistribute land or wealth. He earnestly believed that an open democracy would bring prosperity to the Mexican people, but because of his background, he lacked the ability to appreciate the country's real problems.

---

[134] Ibid, p. 36.
[135] Hansen, p. 27.

Francisco I. Madero. Courtesy El Paso Public Library.

Madero's greatest and first hope, he wrote in *La Sucesión Presidencial en 1910,* was that the vice-president would be chosen in a democratic manner rather than simply named as a presidential appointee. The book was sensible enough to meet with his family's approval: He used the first pages to extol the virtues of Díaz, and expounded on the well-used praises of the constitution of 1857. In subsequent chapters, Madero pointed out that under Díaz, the states had lost the right to elect their own governors, jefes políticos were appointed and so on. He was reiterating an old theme: *Continuismo* created by Díaz was a direct contradiction to Díaz the statesmen.[136]

The moderates of 1908 were not yet the revolutionaries of 1910. They held a world view not dissimilar to the *Porfiristas*. It was the PLM, the exiled Flores Magón brothers had created, who first addressed the problems of mass poverty in Mexico and, in doing so, gathered the

---

[136] Madero, *Francisco, La Sucesión Presidencial en 1910*, as reprinted in Meléndez, José T., *La Revolución Mexicana, Tomo II* (México: Unión Cooperativa de Artes Gráficas del D. F., 1940), pp. 60, 73-76 and 83, 84.

kindling that fueled the entire revolution. That revolution was fought by the poor, illiterate masses, and the PLM alone believed it should be fought for them.

John Kenneth Turner and Ethel Duffy Turner. Courtesy http://www.bicentenario.gob.mx.

Whenever he could, Ricardo Flores Magón was still making noise. Early in 1908, the editor of the *Los Angeles Examiner* sent John Kenneth Turner to interview Ricardo in the Los Angeles jail where he awaited trial for violation of US neutrality laws. Turner, according to his wife, was already a "fiery socialist," but was skeptical, especially about the exile's account of slavery in the Yucatan. In *Barbarous Mexico*, Turner describes his first response to the charges:

"Slavery? Do you mean to tell me there is any real slavery left in the Western Hemisphere?" I scoffed. "Bah, you are talking like an American socialist."[137]

Turner may have written that line to separate in the reader's mind from the American socialist, even though he was one. When he interviewed the three PLM leaders in the Los Angeles jail, Job Harriman, their attorney, made the arrangements for the interview. The socialists of Los Angeles adopted the PLM cause. When one of their richest members, Elizabeth Trowbridge, offered to post bond for the junta members, Los Angeles officials refused the money. Trowbridge, who eventually married Manuel Sarabía, became the biggest source of finances for the exiled junta and for John Turner's journey to Mexico.[138]

---

[137] Turner, Ethel Duffy, in interview with Ruth Teiser, (1966) the Regional Oral History Office of the Bancroft Library, UC Berkeley; Turner, John Kenneth, *Barbarous Mexico* (Austin: Austin University press, reprinted in 1975), p. 5.
[138] Ibid.

Chapter 8

Mexico in the headlines

When historians write about John Kenneth Turner, they usually refer to *Barbarous Mexico*, and it certainly is a tour-de-force of reporting. He had travelled to Mexico in the fall of 1907 with Lazaro Gutiérrez De Lara, who was already a wanted man in Mexico. Turner was in Mexico for a brief time, spent about a week on the Yucatan and another week in Valle Nacional. He returned to the United States and traveled to New York, where the *American Magazine* agreed to publish his articles, provided he return to Mexico and, as his wife put it, "add the political side." So, he returned to Mexico and went to work as the sports editor of the *Mexican Herald*, an English language newspaper, and gained access to the upper crust of Mexico City. He went as far as serving as referee for an international tennis tournament in that city.[139]

What Turner found in Mexico shocked the American public. His book opens with his interview of Ricardo Flores Magón, Antonio Villarreal and Juan Sarabía in the Los Angeles jail. They are not identified in the first chapter of his book, which was drawn from his articles. Although one of the final chapters is dedicated to the junta, the name of Flores Magón is not mentioned in the book until page 151, where he tells the story of a man being shot to death simply for yelling "Viva Ricardo Flores Magon." (The lack of an accent

---

[139] Turner, Ethel Duffy, in interview with Ruth Teiser, (1966) the Regional Oral History Office of the Bancroft Library, UC Berkeley, available on line at https://archive.org/details/cabeuroh_000119, accessed July 11, 2016.

here is the way he wrote Don Ricardo's name – one of the reasons De Lara was so important on his first journey was Turner's lack of Spanish).

He had gone to Mexico looking for slavery and he found it. First, in the Yucatan and then in Valle Nacional. The Mexican plantation owners had worked to keep foreigners out of the henequen trade, but in the Panic of 1907, which created a huge financial crisis, they were willing to talk to a potential American buyer through his interpreter. He learned that the planters paid $65 (US) for each Yaqui delivered to them, the going rate between planters had been $1,000 per able body, but prices were down to $400 when he arrived.[140] Things were worse in the Valle Nacional.

> The planters do not call their slaves slaves. They call them contract laborers. I call them slaves because the moment they enter Valle Nacional they become the personal property of the planters and there is no law or government to protect them."

In the Valle Nacional, Turner found bargains, and he was not afraid of naming names. He quoted a slave dealer:

> The fact that I am the brother-in-law of Felix Díaz [the nephew of Porfirio and who would later be one of the people responsible for the *Decena Trágica*], as well as a personal friend of the governors of the states of Oaxaca and a Veracruz, and the mayors of the cities of the same name... I am prepared to offer you any number of laborers – up to 40,000 a year, men, women and children.

The trader recommended children, because they lived longer, and if the company "adopted" them legally, they could retain them until the age of 22.[141]

[140] Turner, pp. 18,19.
[141] Ibid, p. 107.

Turner also described the situation of the poor, both in the countryside and in the cities. He predicted the United States would gladly go to war to keep Díaz, or a similar administration in power, simply because the Unites States had $900 million invested in Mexico, and sweetheart deals with American monopolies like Standard Oil. William Randolph Hearst owned millions of acres in Northern Mexico.[142]

In the later section of the book, Turner accused the *American Magazine* of being a subject to the Díaz-US Press Conspiracy. The magazine had published his first two articles, then began to edit them heavily and then stopped publication altogether. Ethel Duffy Turner opined in her 1966 interview that somebody bought the magazine. In *Barbarous Mexico*, Turner wrote that after his original material was published, subsequent articles always contained suggestions that Díaz was not personally responsible for any of the problems in Mexico. In a footnote, Turner also accused the *American Magazine* of stealing and printing some of his work with another person's byline.[143]

Although Turner's ties to the PLM affected his work, he brought his own perspective to Mexico and viewed the events and situations differently than did the "independent press" of Mexico. For instance, he referred to *Diario del Hogar* as "old and conservative daily paper." As a member of the working press of Mexico City, he knew what was going on, but most of the journalists who attracted Turner's attention were dead or dying:

> In 1907, the writer Agustín Y Tovao died of poison, administered in Belen. Jesús Martinez Carrion, a noted newspaper artist, and Alberto Arans, a writer,

---

[142] Ibid, p. 135.
[143] Turner, Ethel Duffy, in interview with Ruth Teiser, (1966) the Regional Oral History Office of the Bancroft Library, UC Berkeley, available on line at https://archive.org/details/cabeuroh_000119, accessed July 11,12, 2016; Turner, pp. 238-239.

left Belen to die in a hospital. Dr. Juan de la Pena, editor of a liberal [paper], died in the prison of San Juan de Ulúa... Daniel Cabrera, one of the oldest liberal editors, was a cripple and many times was carried to jail on a stretcher.[144]

Turner held views like those of the unsubsidized Mexican Press about persecution of journalists, but his coverage of the treatment of the Indians differed greatly. While Turner was investigating the use and mistreatment of Yaqui Indians as slaves in Southern Mexico, Silvestre Terrazas covered the latest flare-up in the ongoing conflict between the Indians and the *Federales*. Clearly unsympathetic to the Indians, Don Silvestre reported that 3,000 to 4,000 armed men were in Torreón, ready to take the field against the tribe and noted that even US officials in Washington D.C. were concerned with the problem.[145]

The *New York Times* frequently published articles about the Yaqui wars based on reports from the Mexican Press, but Turner's sympathetic reporting of the plight of the Indians would be unavailable to most American readers for another year. By that time, the Indians who remained would be swept up in the Revolution. They had nothing to lose, and their strongest advocates were in US jails and prisons.

---

[144] Turner, p. 143.
[145] Turner, p. 159; *El Correo de Chihuahua*, May 26, June 26 and July 7, 1908.

Chapter 9

The End of the Beginning and the Beginning of the End

Everything changed in the afternoon of August 23, 1907. A single event precipitated a change in Ricardo Flores Magón, the Mexican Revolution and the attitude of US citizens toward that revolution. In large part, Don Ricardo's impact on the Revolution was behind him, but some of his finest and well-known writing was still ahead of him, as well as hard times and martyrdom, although it would never be completely clear who his sacrifice was for. It is hard to ascertain motivation for change through the veil of time. It could have been age, love, money – and certainly all of those played a part – but it began with Thomas Furlong kicking in his door.

Furlong and his detective agency had been tracking the Flores Magón brothers and their cohorts for years, from San Antonio to St. Louis to Canada and finally to California. Furlong had two of his men with him, as well as two members of the Los Angeles Police Department. He ascertained the writers of *Regeneración* worked at night and stayed out of sight in the day time. He was after Don Ricardo, Librado Rivera and Antonio I. Villarreal. The exact charges were indistinct, but then again, Furlong did not have a warrant or legal authority. But those are details. As he recorded the arrest:

At five o'clock in on the evening of the 23rd (August 1907), we surrounded the cabin. I had with my two Los Angeles Police officers and two of my own men. We found Villarreal and Magón asleep, and Rivera sitting in a chair, also in slumberland, although he was supposed to be on guard at the back door. Our appearance had been so quietly arranged that the parties were complete taken by surprise and did not have time to reach their arms. They fought hard, however, and continued to struggle all the way from the cabin to the jail, a distance of at least three miles. A wagon happened to pass the place at the time and I pressed it into service, and it kept us busy to keep the prisoners in the wagon, as they struggled and fought the entire distance, and kept up a continual squawking, which reminded on of a flock of wild geese. None of them spoke English, and the only things they could were that they were being kidnapped and the words "help" and "liberales" ... We landed them safely in the city prison, and without anyone sustaining serious injury, except a few teeth knocked out, bruised faces and black eyes.[146]

Furlong acknowledged the fact that he did not have a warrant later in court, and boasted to a Los Angeles newspaper that he had captured 180 Mexican dissidents and turned them over to the Díaz government – an ironic statement for a man who illegally arrested three others for violation of US neutrality laws.[147]

For the next three years, Don Ricardo would be confined – first in Los Angeles, then in Arizona, while Mexico drifted toward explosion. He and his companions were the impetus for the Turner expedition and were incarcerated when the Creelman interview went public and sent Francisco Madero on his rise to power. He had estranged the reformist of

---

[146] Furlong, p. 142.
[147] Turner, p. 291.

Mexico, the people who wanted the end of *Continuismo*, when he had basically usurped the PLM with the proclamation of 1906 and made himself the PLM president.

Economics, as always, played a part in public and private history. The Panic of 1907 had hit Mexico hard, but in an unbalanced manner. The *Mestizos*, who had enjoyed a modicum of financial gain during the Porfiriato, saw that slipping away. The *Cientificos* and *Hacendados* were still overly affluent, given to European vacations, and imported foreign goods (causing a decrease in domestic production). The Indians were as desperate as ever. The personal finances of Ricardo Flores Magón depended more and more on the American left. He had been in contact with Emma Goldman, the fire-brand anarchist who would eventually be deported to the Soviet Union, and the socialist lawyer Job Harriman, who took on the case brought by Furlong. For the rest of his life, Don Ricardo found himself more closely linked with the fringe left in the United States than the revolutionaries of Mexico – even though in the opening battles, many fought for him.[148]

PLM Fiat Money. Courtesy Archivo Magón.

---

[148] Hansen, p. 28; Lomnitz p.252.

Ricardo Flores Magón and Maria Broussé.
Courtesy Archivo Magón

And somewhere along the way, Don Ricardo had found love. Her name was María Talavera Broussé. Six years older than Don Ricardo, she had a daughter whom he adopted and adored. The letters between Ricardo and María are the stuff of romance and rebellion and they could easily go from love to revolution in the same sentence. He addressed her as "María of my soul" and would end his letters with kisses for both María and her daughter, Lucia. In turn, she would complain about sleepless nights away from him.[149]

Don Ricardo did not view himself as apathetic and tried to be active. With the help of Maria and Ethel Duffy Turner, he smuggled plans for the revolution of 1908 out of the jail. He slipped a piece of paper through metal grate when the guard went to the end of the hall. María picked it up when she reached for her purse, that motion blocked the guards view as she hid the paper in her large skirts fashionable at that time, she and Ethel were wearing. The women gave the paper to a messenger who took it across the border, but the Díaz administration had found a convict in Torreon who resembled Antonio Villarreal, who went to the border, got the paper and turned it over to the authorities. "That," Ethel said, "was how the revolution of 1908 was betrayed."[150]

María was not the only person he wrote to. Other letters showed a slow transformation in his approach to revolution. On June 13, he wrote to his brother Enrique and Práxedis Guerrero, a trusted associate (who gave his life at a skirmish in Palomas, Chihuahua, before Don Ricardo's release from prison):

> The rich would rebel if there would be an attempt put into practice the Program of the *Partido Liberal Mexicano,* if, by a true and unique miracle in the history of popular revolutions, the ideals of the revolution would remain intact after the triumph... As anarchists, we know all of this well ...to obtain great benefits for the people, it's necessary to work as well-disguised anarchists, even from those who take us as leaders. Everything boils down to a mere question of tactics. From the start, if we had called ourselves

---

[149] Ricardo Flores Magón to Maria Broussé, September 27, 1908, as published in *Epistolario y Textos de Ricardo Flores Magón* (México: Fondo de Cultura Económica, 1964), pp. 178-179, 166-167.
[150] Ethel Duffy Turner interview 1966.

anarchist from the start, no one, not even a few, would have listened. Without calling ourselves anarchists, no one, not even a few, would have listened. Without calling ourselves anarchists we've been placing in men's mind thought of hate against the possessing class and against the governmental caste.[151]

During the abortive, eighth edition run of *El Hijo de Ahuizote* in 1902, Don Ricardo used private funds to have 2000 copies of Peter Kropotkin's *The Conquest of Bread* translated, printed and distributed in Mexico, but he did not wave the anarchist flag in print. He understood both the Mexican and American mindset. Economic necessity pushed him from the milieu of Mexican society into the maelstrom of the American left. His lawyer, Job Harriman, was a leading socialist, and Turner was an ardent socialist. Emma Goldman was an anarchist, and then there were the communists. These political types were anxious to take on the "Mexican cause," personified in Ricardo Flores Magón. Unfortunately, his ties to the American left would eventually but effectively reduce his influence on the outcome of Mexican Revolution.

In 1909, while Don Ricardo sat in jail, venting his frustration, Don Porfirio had other things on his mind. He had quashed the magazine articles by Turner that would later become *Barbarous Mexico*, and was preparing for both the election of 1910 – in his mind a given - and for the centennial of Hidalgo's revolt of 1810 that triggered Mexican independence. As the economic plight of many Mexicans grew, Díaz built his favors with investors using American journalists. To this end, he used the administration's favorite tool: bribery. Díaz made substantial gifts to several American reporters and hired James Creelman outright.

---

[151] Ricardo Flores Magón to Enrique Flores Magón and Práxedis, Guerrero July 13, 1908, as translated by Chaz Bufe in *Dreams of Freedom,* p. 112.

Gratuities went to Harrison Gray Otis, publisher of the *Los Angeles Times*, who owned land on the Baja peninsula, and to William Randolph Hearst, who owned one of the largest ranches in Chihuahua.[152]

A series of articles that ran in *Sunset*, a magazine John Turner claimed to be owned by the Southern Pacific Railroad, typified the pro- Díaz propaganda. *Sunset* editors justified the series, "Mexico as it is," because of the forthcoming elections but never mentioned any candidate except Díaz. An anonymous socialite of Mexico City supposedly wrote the articles, which began appearing in February, 1910, and spared no accolade to Díaz:

> Even though President Díaz has expressed his desire to withdraw from power and to rest – the people have acclaimed him a candidate for the coming presidential term, and with also Señor Corral, to continue as vice-president. With this popular informal nomination, Mexico has demonstrated that she is resolved not to abandon for a moment, the program of peace and progress which General Díaz carried out with such remarkable results.[153]

The *Sunset* ran the series for three months. The magazine published an article in May, explaining that the Yaquis, blood-thirsty killers that they were, had to be deported to the Yucatan for the safety of the Mexican populace. The author praised the tactic and claimed it had been successful. The Yaquis, he wrote, had been pacified because of fear of deportation. They were no longer being shipped to the state of Yucatan where the transplanted Indians now "stand in the same relationship to their employers as the rest of the field laborers in that state."[154]

---

[152] Turner, Ethel Duffy, p. 13; personal interview with Jane Dale Lloyd.
[153] Gonzales, Gaspar Estrada, "Mexico As It Is," *Sunset Magazine,* Volume 24, January-June, 1910, pp. 73-74.
[154] Ibid.

Nothing had changed for the Yaquis or Mexico, but the *Porfirian* propaganda against the Turner articles, and the efforts to publicize the case against Ricardo Flores Magón had intensified the pressure on the internal opposition press of Mexico. Meanwhile, Don Ricardo had problems of his own, both romantically and politically. On January 9, 1909, he wrote María, "Do you know how I suffer from the lack of letters? Horrible suffering." He was also concerned that she remained a member of the Socialist Party, which could mean divided loyalties. He also questioned the trustworthiness of Lazaro Gutierrez de Lara, the man who initially led Turner into Mexico.

Although Don Ricardo would not publicly acclaim his allegiance to anarchism until his release in 1910, his years of being hounded by government operatives of two countries, and his time in the jails and prisons of both countries had made him extremely cynical about the nature of all governments, and he was both paranoid and pragmatic. He advised María that it would not be a good idea to separate from "the Americans", referring to John Murray, and the Turners, who were putting out a short-lived socialist magazine called *The Border*. The magazine offered up a romanticized version of the Mexican cause, and was funded by Elizabeth Trowbridge, who ended up marrying Manuel Sarabía, the one dissident she was able to bust out of jail for health reasons. The two would eventual run away from North America to live in London. The American supporters of the Ricardo Flores Magón faction had to fend for themselves as a result.[155] Manuel's tuberculosis would eventually kill him.[156]

---

[155] Ricardo Flores Magón to Maria Broussé, January 31, 1909, Maria Broussé, September 27, as published *in Epistolario y Textos de Ricardo Flores Magón* (México: Fondo de Cultura Económica, 1964), p.193.
[156] Lomnitz, p. 177.

The Junta of the PLM in 1910. From left: Anselmo Figueroa, Práxedis Guerrero, Ricardo Flores Magón (seated), Enrique Flores Magón, and Librado Rivera. Práxedis' face has been superimposed onto that of another central figure in the PLM, most likely Antonio Villarreal, who by then had broken with the group. (Courtesy *El Hijo de Ahuizote*)

Don Ricardo ultimately realized that his efforts could only realistically be supported by the radicals on the northern side of the border. Even though he wrote María, "I no longer have any faith except in the people. I don't believe in any one else." His future conflicts with former colleagues – particularly Juan Sarabía and Antonio Villarreal would bear this out. However, in a cursory look at the regenerated *Regeneración* indicates an influx of both money and staff. While its creators continued to live in poverty, offices and the photographic process came dear, and after 1910, the newspaper would reflect not only the Mexican cause but the activities of all entities on the extreme left.

The anti-reelection party of Mexico formally nominated Francisco I. Madero for president in April 1910. On May 29, representatives of the independent newspapers of Mexico City met to endorse him. Filomeno Mata was absent, serving yet another jail sentence, but a son and daughter represented him. They carried a placard with *Diario Del*

Hogar scrawled in large black letters denoting mourning. Afterwards, newspapermen and members of the Mata family carried the placard to the National Palace as a sign of protest, but to no avail.[157]

As the election drew near, the regime increased its persecution of the anti-re-electionist movement. In an open letter to Díaz, Madero complained:

> In Coahuila, the public officials have arbitrarily forbidden demonstrations in our honor, preventing also the spread of our principles. The same happened in the states of Nuevo Leon, Aguascalientes and San Luis Potosí... In the states of Sonora and Puebla the conditions are serious. In the former, an independent journalist, Mr. Caesar del Vando, was thrown into jail... At Cananea the prosecutions are extreme against members of my party, and according to late news received there more than 30 individuals have been imprisoned, among them the full board of directors of the *Club Anti-Reeleccionista de Obreros,* three of whom were forcibly enlisted in the army.
>
> At Puebla, Atlixco and Tlaxcala, where untold outrages have been committed against my followers, intense excitement is raised. The last news received shows the condition of the working class to be desperate; they may at any moment resort to violent means to have their rights respected.[158]

The letter contains two interesting aspects: First, when Madero refers to the "spread our principles," he is talking simply about the end of *Continuismo*, nothing more. Land distribution or wealth distribution never was nor ever would be a significant part of his agenda. The candidate for the presidency, who pursued his quest within the rules of the

---

[157] Mata, p. 85.
[158] Turner, John, p. 165

existing structure, still was a reformer, not a revolutionary. His followers, for the most part, were people who could benefit economically from the reforms he was proposing, in large part simply by unlocking the chokehold the *Cientificos* had on the government. Secondly, Madero, who had taken graduate courses in agriculture at the University of California at Berkeley, was known to have treated his own workers well. Despite this fact, the welfare of the working classes of Mexico was less his concern, and certainly not the concern of his followers. *Indios* did not receive much of a consideration among the anti-re-electionists, since they did not vote.

The Díaz regime, working through state governors, persecuted journalists, who openly supported Madero because they made the easiest targets. As early as October 1909, José María Pino Suarez complained in a letter to *Diario Del Hogar* that more than 100 newspapermen nationwide had been imprisoned under false pretenses and that at least 50 others had been conscripted into the Mexican army.[159]

This was not the most prudent move for an administration that was about to face armed violence from all sides, especially since it was common practice for the Mexican army to lock its soldiers into barracks at night to keep them from running away.[160] Invisible lines were being drawn in the sand, and some of those lines had been drawn in the first decade of the 20th century by the Flores Magón brothers. Things were changing quickly. Ricardo Flores Magón was getting out of jail, and Madero was going in.

Madero's candidacy proved too much for Díaz. On June 6, a month before the scheduled election, he had Madero arrested in Monterrey. By this one act, Díaz succeeded in a task that Don Ricardo had failed to accomplish. He turned

---

[159] *Diario del Hogar*, October 19, 1909
[160] Personal conversation with independent researcher Heribert von Feilitzsch, March 16, 2016.

Francisco Madero into a revolutionary. Ironically, Díaz probably would have handily won the election. The force that rose against him in future months would not use the ballot.

Chapter 10

The Illusion Unravels

War requires both rage and money. Porfirio Díaz had the money, the people who revolted against him had the rage. Eventually, money would make the difference, but where did the rage come from?

On September 16, 1910, Mexico celebrated a century of independence from Spain – actually, that was the centennial of the abortive Hidalgo uprising. The president, who had been elected "unanimously," was busy unveiling monuments (some of which still stand today) and entertaining the diplomatic corps that came to pay tribute to the "maker of modern Mexico."

Not surprisingly, on June 16, 1910, Díaz had Madero arrested in Monterrey for insulting the president and fomenting revolution. Equally unsurprising was the fact that, when the election was held 12 days later, he lost. The results of that election have varied in historical reports, but in a nation of between 11 and 15 million people, almost 19,000 people voted for Díaz and less than 250 voted for Madero. Of course, more than 5,000 *anti-re-electionists* had been jailed, Don Francisco had merely been the most prominent.[161]

The electoral "triumph" of Díaz in Chihuahua was typical: a handful people, nine in Ciudad Juárez and 16 in Batopilas, voted for Francisco I. Madero, even though he had been removed from the ballot. In Cd. Juárez, election officials told voters that Madero was not an eligible candidate. In

---

[161] Knight, Volume I, p. 75.

Batopilas, the police jailed the leader of the club *anti-releccionista*. On September 16, Díaz reported to the Mexican legislature that he had won the election.[162]

Being in a Mexican jail, then as now, is not too bad if one is rich, and after the election, Madero's father was able to post a bond that allowed allow his son to ride horseback around San Luis Potosí where he was being confined. On October 5, Francisco Madero simply galloped away from his guards, concealed himself in the baggage car of a train going north, and arrived in San Antonio, Texas. There he issued the *Plan de San Luis* Potosí -- also dated Oct. 5 – his last day in Mexico, because in the unwritten rules of Mexican revolt, revolutionaries had to have a plan and it had to be issued from Mexico.[163]

The fraudulent elections did not diminish the ardor as celebrators in Mexico City honored Díaz. To the foreign visitors, the capital displayed, at least on the surface, the modernity and affluence that had become associated with the Díaz regime: new electric street lights had been installed for the occasion, the national palace, the Cathedral and the Plaza de Constitución were illuminated. *Presidente* and Señora Díaz sponsored a "garden party" a Chapultepec Castle, and banners proclaiming "Peace, Liberty and Progress" hung above the well-lit streets.[164]

The US press covered the celebrations with a pro- Díaz bias. The *New York Times* published a - for American papers - typical article by an unnamed special correspondent:

---

[162] Alameda, Francisco R, *La Revolución en Estado de Chihuahua*, Tomo I (Chihuahua: Chihuahua de la Revolución Mexicana, 1964), p. 158; Ross, p.107.
[163] There are various accounts of Madero's escape, this happens to be my personal favorite.
[164] García, Genaro, "Las Fiestas del Centenario" from *Crónica Oficial de las fiestas del primer centenario de la Independencia de México*, as reprinted *in La Revolución Mexicana*, pp. 205-207.

Mexico's celebration of the 100th anniversary of martyred Father Hidalgo's proclamation of independence has been coupled with an equally impressive celebration of the eightieth anniversary of that wonderful old man, Porfirio Díaz. Who can doubt the supposedly lesser includes the seemingly greater? Mexico's centennial of independence is unquestionably another manifestation of the power of its president... One's first impression of President Díaz justifies the idea formed of him in reading. Short of stature physically, his personality is large. He stands erect, he walks briskly. His face in repose is grave and stern, but it lights up wonderfully when he is greeting a visitor he is glad to see, or discussing a subject that interests him... he goes about daily in his limousine unguarded. At the National Palace soldiers surround him, but he fearlessly exposes himself. Probably he has no cause for fear...[165]

To the United States, Madero's attempt to become president were "the ravings of a mad man" and had become an historical anachronism. The *Times* special correspondent wrote:

Poor Madero, under surveillance somewhere far from the capital, has his admirers. There were cries for him in the densely-crowded streets last night. The *Rurales* soon silenced the cries and placed the patriots who uttered them where they could sleep off the effects of too much tequila or mescal... but as a matter of fact there is no real opposition to Díaz, organized or unorganized. While he retains power, the prosperity of the country will remain unchecked by any outbreak of revolutionary spirit so strong in

---

[165] *New York Times*, September 24, 1910.

the Latin blood, and foreign enterprise, so needful in the development of the country, will be protected.[166]

As Don Francisco trotted around San Luis Potosí, making his plans, Ricardo Flores Magón, Librado Rivera and Antonio Villarreal were released from prison at Florence, Arizona, on August 3. They boarded a train for Los Angeles, where they were greeted by hundreds of people. There were speeches at a local union hall that evening, but the main attraction was John Kenneth Turner, who had become famous because of his exposure of the Díaz regime, and was more famous than the PLM junta.[167]

Regeneración rose again on September 3, but with major differences. This time, calling itself *Seminal Revolucionario* (Revolutionary Weekly), the fourth and last page broadsheet newspaper was entirely in English. For the first time, the publication contained photos – two photographs on page two of the Junta's reception at the train station. This is significant because placing photos in newspapers was a time consuming and expensive process in those days. In the Spanish section appeared signed articles by Don Ricardo, Práxedis Guerrero and Antonio Villarreal. The return of *Regeneración*, for the fourth time, was explained on page one. Page four featured a bad translation into English by the German socialist Alfred G. Sanftleben, who sprinkled the strange phrase, "here we go again," into the article. But whether in Spanish or English, the articles represented a call to war.[168]

There were other notable changes. In both Spanish and English, advertisements offered both, subscriptions (two US

---

[166] Trowbridge, E.D., *Mexico To-Day and To-Morrow*, (New York: Macmillan Company, 1919) p. 132; *New York Times*, September 24, 1910.
[167] Bufe, Verter, p. 354.
[168] Ibid; *Regeneración*, September 3,1910, accessed from *The Anarchist Annals of Ricardo Flores Magón* (http://archivomagon.net/periodicos/regeneracion-1900-1918/2da-epoca), accessed July 20, 2016.

dollars or five Mexican pesos per year) and bundles – 100 papers for $3.75, 500 for $15 and 1,000 copies for $20 – those rates were not given in Spanish.

The paper also, both in English and in Spanish, printed the party platform of the *Partido Liberal Mexicano*. This was basically a reiteration of the document the Junta had produced in 1906, but it was "signed" both in Spanish and in English, by the Junta, with their titles: Ricardo Flores *Magón*, president; Juan Sarabía, vice-president (even though at this time, Sarabía was incarcerated in Mexico City); Antonio I Villarreal, secretary; Enrique Flores Magón, treasurer; Librado Rivera, first speaker; and Manuel Sarabía, second speaker.

The document is historically interesting for two reasons. First, the relationships of the individuals involved would change greatly in the coming conflict. Second, while the platform is merely a re-iteration of the PLM proclamation of 1906 (Don Ricardo had yet to show his true political colors as an anarchist), it dealt with specific policies: It sought to limit not only the power of the president, but also of the Church, demanded the guarantee of human rights, and promoted public education.[169]

This was in stark contrast to the *Plan de San Luis Potosí*, which Madero had conceived in confinement or in exile in San Antonio. Don Francisco seems to have taken some cues from Thomas Jefferson and the American Declaration of Independence as he outlined his indictment of Porfirio Díaz:

> Peoples, in their constant efforts for the triumph of the ideal of liberty and justice, are forced, at precise historical moments, to make their greatest sacrifices.
>
> Our beloved country has reached one of those moments. A force of tyranny which we Mexicans

---

[169] Ibid.

were not accustomed to suffer after we won our independence oppresses us in such a manner that it has become intolerable. In exchange for that tyranny we are offered peace, but peace full of shame for the Mexican nation, because its basis is not law, but force; because its object is not the aggrandizement and prosperity of the country, but to enrich a small group who, abusing their influence, have converted the public charges into fountains of exclusively personal benefit, unscrupulously exploiting the manner of lucrative concessions and contracts.

From this it results that the whole administrative, judicial, and legislative machinery obeys a single will, the caprice of General Porfirio, who during his long administration has shown that the principal motive that guides him is to maintain himself in power and at any cost.[170]

The Mexican government had formally charged Madero with insulting authorities and fomenting a revolution. Inadvertently it turned him into something he abhorred, a violent revolutionary, something he would never be good at. Ricardo Flores Magón, had been calling for a violent revolution for six years. He also proved rather inept at the task. The one man, who had proven his ability as a violent revolutionary, Porfirio Díaz, was as detached from the economic realities as his two sworn enemies.

For all of September 1910, Díaz reigned over his self-congratulatory celebration. But Mexican prosperity, like the *Pax Porfiriana*, was an illusion. The decline of silver prices, the world depression of 1907 and subsequent drops in demands for Mexican exports all affected Mexico's ailing economy. The international popularity of Díaz had resulted largely from his payment of the international debt accumulated in the 19th century. During the last few years

---

[170] Madero, Francisco, *El Plan de San Luis Potosí*, as translated by the Modern History Source book of Fordham University.

of his regime, rampant inflation seriously affected price of basic staples. The Mexican government found itself threatened on two fronts: The country's international financial credibility was in danger, and the poor and middle classes were becoming, understandably, discontent. As the celebration continued, the Mexican finance minister José Yves Limantour, traveled to Europe to renegotiate Mexico's foreign debt.[171]

Díaz, Madero and Ricardo Flores Magón all seemed oblivious to Mexico's financial problems. In the eighth paper to be printed in Los Angeles, *Regeneración* featured a front-page article "*Madero en Estado Unidos*" (Madero in the United States), but since its newest inception, several major changes were noticeable in the newspaper. It featured signed articles, generally a rousing editorial from Don Ricardo on page one, such as "*El Derecho de Rebelión*" *(the right to rebel)*, while the English page, at least at first, featured messages to the proletariat, but also features from John Turner – taken from his book. There were some obvious and not-so-obvious problems with the English page: Sanftleben had policy differences with the Junta and soon departed. According to Verter in *Dreams of Freedom, a Ricardo Flores Magón Reader*, the approach of a real shooting war helped Don Ricardo clearly define his goals of "human freedom" but also in pragmatic language that addressed logistical concerns. The edition that carried the news of Madero's arrival also marked the appearance of Ethel Duffy Turner on the English page. News of Madero's arrival was not published on the English page.[172]

In 1966, an 82-year-old Ethel D. Turner recalled one of the proudest moments of her youth in October of 1910: She and

[171] Trowbridge, p. 132; *New York Times*, September 24, 1910; Cumberland, pp. 13-14.
[172] *Regeneración*, various issues, September 10 through November 28, 1910, accessed from *The Anarchist Annals of Ricardo Flores Magón* (http://archivomagon.net/periodicos/regeneracion-1900-1918/2da-epoca), accessed July 20, 2016; Bufe, Verter, p. 75.

her husband were called into the offices of the Junta and informed of the date of the revolution: November 20. Whether this represented an agreement between the Junta and Madero is not known, but it was announced in the following edition of *Regeneración*. Rather than thousands of rebels taking on the federal army all over Mexico, the "revolution" fizzled with only a few flare ups of violence in remote areas of Mexico. On November 20, *El Correo de Chihuahua* published the headline, "Madero in in Laredo, Texas," but the following day, the lead story concerned efforts of the Mexican government to have Madero extradited. The paper published an update on November 22, under the headline, "the delicate situation," and two days later, the largest (yet inaccurate) headline yet: "Madero in Coahuila." On November 23, Enrique Creel, now ambassador to the United States, told the *New York Times*, the revolution had been "crushed."[173]

As happens in many wars, the beginning was less than ostentatious. Madero crossed the border as promised on November 20, but finding no army to meet him, he retreated across the Rio Grande. Aquiles Serdán, a shoe salesman in Puebla, is often credited with firing the first shot of the Mexican Revolution. When Puebla police went to arrest him, a member of the *Club Anti-reeleccionista*, at his home on November 18, opened fire. Police and *Federales* killed the family and discovered a cache of arms and ammunition. *El Imparcial* in Mexico City reported these events the next day under the banner headline *"Viva Gen. Díaz!"* (Hurray for General Díaz).[174]

The revolutionary flames flickered and almost died. Madero, who had moved his staff to New Orleans, was disheartened. In Los Angeles, Don Ricardo, a veteran of crumbling revolts, moved on, ever closer to the left, which soon brought him

---

[173] Ethel Duffy Turner, 1966 interview; *El Correo de Chihuahua*, November 21,21,22,23, and 24, 1910; *New York Times*, November 23, 1910.
[174] *El Imparcial*, November 19, 1910.

into open conflict with his closest supporters. The Díaz regime moved ahead with brutal oppression in apparent self-content. Something that Don Ricardo had realized years before and that Francisco Madero was realizing now, the rage came before the money, was driven externally, but exploded internally. But first, the *Porfirian* regime struck out blindly, like a rattlesnake blinded by the shedding of its skin.

In November, Mexican authorities arrested Filomeno Mata and his son, Filomeno Jr., the editor of *Diario Del Hogar*, for defaming a minor official. From his prison cell, the old man wrote his last editorial, "no re-election was a debt." He traced the history of the Díaz regime and pointed out that Díaz opposed the very cause he had trumpeted in his rise to power. Mata concluded, "It is time. The people want the freedom to choose their own successor." Filomeno Mata died in Veracruz, his health broken by Belen, less than a year later.[175]

Agents of the Chihuahua state government arrested Silvestre Terrazas on November 26, at his offices at *Correo De Chihuahua*. Police took him first to the state prison where he was held incommunicado for several days, then transferred without a judicial order to Lecumberri prison, known as the "black Palace," in Mexico City (Today the National Archives of Mexico). The exact charges are unknown, but his daughter claimed he was arrested for publishing the complete *Plan de San Luis Potosí*, which he clearly had not (nobody in Mexico had). In fact, his objective coverage of the Madero revolt demonstrated that Don Silvestre was not yet a *Maderista*. His ongoing editorial bias had not been against Díaz, but against the Terrazas-Creel power structure in Chihuahua. The logical assumption is that Don Luis preferred him out of the way during the coming tumult.

---

[175] Mata, pp. 88-89.

The rage was already there. A lynch mob in Rock Springs, Texas, burned a Mexican national to death on November 4, setting off a wave of anti-American riots that swept Mexico. The incident generated fervor for the revolutionary cause. In Mexico City, a mob, comprised of both *Maderistas* and *Magonistas*, threw a bomb into the US embassy, then attacked the offices of *El Imparcial* and the *Mexican Herald*. The mob lynched one US citizen, the police killed two demonstrators.[176]

Díaz began concentrating his troops, which left many garrisons deserted or understaffed. This move not only lent credence to the idea of revolution, but also gave rise to violence against those who local residents considered their immediate oppressors in many areas, either the local rich or remaining soldiers. E. D. Trowbridge, an American writer in Mexico during the Revolution, described the adventures of one band, formed by Gabriel Hernández:

> Hernández, an Indian lad of 24 years of age, started with three men at the villages of Chignahuapan, in the state of Puebla, to raise a *Maderista* band. Within a few days, he had picked up fifteen or twenty men from neighboring villages and had obtained horses and arms from sympathizers. It was an easy matter to take possession of several small towns and villages, and in each more recruits were obtained, and farmers were induced to contribute horses "for the cause." The band, all mounted and now numbering a hundred men or more, took the town of Saccaland, a place of considerable importance, then occupied Xico, and then Huachinango, the County Seat.[177]

---

[176] *Regeneración*, various issues, November 12, 1910, accessed from *The Anarchist Annals of Ricardo Flores Magón* (http://archivomagon.net/periodicos/regeneracion-1900-1918/2da-epoca), accessed July 20, 2016.
[177] Trowbridge, pp. 133-134.

The reference to *Maderista* in the forgoing paragraph can honestly be questioned. Americans were familiar with Madero because he received wide spread coverage. If they knew Ricardo Flores Magón at all, it was because they had read *Barbarous Mexico*. As Ethel Duffy Turner pointed out in her 1966 interview, many more people had read the initial American magazine articles than the book – and Don Ricardo had not been mentioned in those articles. As for the Mexicans, particularly like the "Indian lad" mentioned above, they were living in a population where the highest estimate of literate people was less than 20 percent. Most of them did not know the difference between Flores Magón and Madero.[178]

Writing in 1912, after Madero had risen to power, Thomas Furlong credited both the Cananea strike and the early stages of the Revolution in 1910 to *Magonistas*, but the actual defeat of Díaz he credited, to

> those parties that stepped in at the opportune time to reap the benefit of the turmoil, disruption that had been created by the Magón faction. This faction was headed by Madero, who had financial means and a somewhat better class of followers than Magón.[179]

The history of the Mexican Revolution, it could be said, would be written by a "better class of followers." Ethel Duffy Turner complained in print years later, that the *Magonistas* fought and won many of the initial battles, but the spoils went to the *Maderistas*. Those battles, like all battles, were fought with more rage than political dogma.[180]

As Mariano Azuela, wrote in his 1916 novel of the Revolution, *The Underdogs*:

> Villa, Obregon, Carranza? What's the difference? I love the revolution like a volcano in eruption. I love

---

[178] Ethel Duffy Turner, 1966 interview; Hansen, pp. 154-155.
[179] Furlong, p. 159.
[180] Turner, Ethel Duffy, p. 217.

the volcano because it's a volcano, the revolution because it's the revolution.[181]

Sometimes that "better class of followers" got caught up in events, like Silvestre Terrazas, who languished in Lecumberri prison from December, 1910 to February, 1911. When he was transferred from Chihuahua to Mexico City, one of the guards who accompanied him was to claim the *ley fuga* (the law of flight) and kill him. He refused the orders that had obviously come from Chihuahua, not from Mexico City.[182]

Don Silvestre's wife followed him to Mexico City and, once there, wrote to Señora Díaz and asked her to intervene. The president agreed to interview the prisoner. Díaz asked him about the situation in Chihuahua, which by February had become the center of revolutionary activities. The newspaper man responded by making a speech against the Terrazas-Creel clan and their various monopolies in the state – not a bad idea given the bad blood between the dictator and the land holding giant. Díaz, believing Don Silvestre represented no threat to his personal image in Chihuahua, had him released. However, one of Don Silvestre's first articles after returning to Chihuahua was an interview with Madero.[183]

Don Silvestre asked Madero if the rift between the *Magonistas* and *Maderistas* was irreparable. Madero replied that it was not certain, but he had stopped worrying about it. He had not had any contact with Don Ricardo since coming to the United States in October, and claimed he did not know why Flores Magón was attacking him in his newspaper.

Madero, in all probability, was lying. The initial phase of the Mexican Revolution had been suppressed as easily as it had quelled the PLM revolts of 1906 and 1908. Both the US

---

[181] Azuela, Mariano, translated by E. Munguía, Jr., *The Underdogs* (Original title, *Los De Abajo*) (New York: Signet, 1962), p. 131.
[182] Terrazas, Margarita, personal interview.
[183] Terrazas, Silvestre, p. 60.

Press and the subsidized press of Mexico declared the emergency over by December.

Chapter 11

No law to abolish Misery

Solo el que sufre sabe comprender al sufre.
(Only he who suffers can understand suffering.)

Ricardo Flores Magón[184]

The rift between Flores Magón and Madero could not be addressed because in Don Ricardo's mind, it never happened. Don Ricardo's vision of revolution had been quite strong since 1906. When hostilities sputtered to a beginning in November, he advised PLM members to fight with the *Maderistas*, but not join them. He believed that a grass roots rebellion would change things in Mexico, and Madero was a minor character, or simply another member of the elite looking for personal power. One of the major questions about Ricardo Flores Magón was what he believed and when he believed it. Librado Rivera, who had worked with the Flores Magón brother since their days of *El Hijo de Ahuizote* wrote in 1922 about their relationship. He remembered Don Ricardo having 2,000 copies of Kropotkin's *Conquest of Bread* printed and distributed in Mexico City in 1902. Of course, by 1900, all the Flores Magón brothers were well-versed in the writings of the major anarchists of the day.

Although Don Ricardo developed ties with Emma Goldman in 1905, there was no written record until 1907 (in a private letter to his closest associates of his allegiance to anarchy),

---

[184] As quoted by Librado Rivera in the prologue to Santillán, Diego Abad de, *Ricardo Flores Magón: El Apóstol de la Revolución Social Mexicana* (México: Grupo Cultura, 1925), p. X.

and he did not go public for being an anarchist until 1911 (in an article in *Regeneración*). Still, Don Ricardo did not base his views on European theory: Both he and his family had suffered from the hand of two governments, and he knew that William C. Owens – *Regeneración's* long-time English editor - was right when he said Mexican peons did not know the difference between socialism, communism and anarchy, and that they didn't care.

For his part, Don Ricardo constantly stated that his goal was not to replace one set of tyrants with another. In his opinion, government was the enemy, and he would and did oppose every government that followed Díaz.[185]

Madero had broken with Ricardo Flores Magón in in 1907, mainly triggered by his abhorrence of violence. Now that Don Francisco found himself in the middle of a shooting war as the Revolution took shape in 1911, he needed Don Ricardo, possibly more than Don Ricardo needed him. The Díaz administration had written off the Cananea strike as a trivial incident, and something that basically had nothing to do with the PLM, beyond, perhaps, inspiration.

There were smaller uprisings throughout Mexico from the summer of 1906 through 1908, again trivialized by Díaz and most historians. However, Madero knew more about that particular situation than Díaz. A 66-page booklet, *Los Precursores de la Revolución*, written by Teodore Hernández in 1944, provides mini biographies of 64 people in 37 different places (there were 12 in Chihuahua alone, where Madero was fighting at the time of his January, 1911 interview with Silvestre Terrazas), and a half dozen in San Luis Potosí, while others spread from Sonora to Veracruz to the Yucatan. After the initial list, Hernandez included about

---

[185] Ibid, pp. X-XI.

twenty more individuals, who, for one reason or another, had been left out of the book.[186]

In one sense, Madero was already indebted to Flores Magón. Pascual Orozco, one of his leading generals – and the one that would be instrumental in winning the war against Díaz, leading to the treaty of Juarez - became radicalized by reading *Regeneración* back in 1908. The former mule-skinner, instead of being just a bandit, became a "bandit with a cause" long before he met Don Francisco.[187]

Regeneración.
Semanal revolucionario

Francisco I. Madero es un Traidor
a la Causa de la Libertad

The February 25, 1911 edition of Regeneración. Courtesy *The Anarchist Annals of Ricardo Flores Magón.*

Madero also knew that his present ally and soon to be opponent, Emiliano Zapata had been reading *Regeneración* since October 1905, the same year that Don Francisco had contributed $1,400 to the Flores Magón activities. Zapata, now one of the most revered revolutionary heroes of Mexico, took the standard editorial ending, "Land and Liberty" as his faction's battle cry. Zapata became a great

---

[186] Hernando, Teodore, *Los Precursores de la Revolución* (México: Sin Editorial, 1944), pp. 6-7.
[187] Buchenau, Jürgen, Gilbert, Joseph M., *Mexico's Once and Future Revolution: Social Upheaval and the Challenge of Rule Since the Late nineteenth Century* (Durham: Duke University Press, 2013). Orozco actually was the owner of a prosperous transportation business and mines, not just a "mule skinner," as most histories defined him.

revolutionary leader, and the favorite of Ricardo Flores Magón.[188]

There were also reasons of a personal nature. Antonio Villarreal had abandoned *Regeneración* and joined Madero in February. Villarreal was one of Flores Magón's most trusted advisers. He took over the paper when the Junta fled to Canada in 1906, and moved the paper to Los Angeles in 1910. The departure must have been rapid and surreptitious as Villarreal had three signed articles in the January 25, 1911 edition. Madero took him in and immediately had him publish a bogus version of *Regeneración* in Chihuahua. The Maderistas also disseminated a circular claiming that Don Ricardo had accepted the position of provisional vice-president (The Maderistas used this ploy again before the national election of 1911, when Madero received 90 percent of the vote).[189]

Ricardo Flores Magón reacted violently to the Terrazas interview. On February 25, he responded with a front-page and signed editorial, headlined, *"Francisco I. Madero es un traidor a la Causa de Libertad"* (Francisco I. Madero is a traitor to the cause of liberty). Madero was closer to Díaz, at least according to Flores Magón:

> Mexicans, open your eyes. Why doesn't Madero fight with *el Partido Liberal*? Because *El Partido Liberal* fights for the poor, whose interests are opposite those of the rich... The rich need the poor to work and for this Madero will not support *el Partido Liberal*

---

[188] Ricardo Flores Magón to Francisco Madero, March 5, 1905, as republished in *Obras Completas* in http://archivomagon.net/biblioteca-digital/, accessed July 22, 2016; Bufe, Verter, *Dreams of Freedom,* p. 345.
[189] *Regeneración*, January 25, and various editions in March and April, 1911, accessed from *The Anarchist Annals of Ricardo Flores Magón* (http://archivomagon.net/periodicos/regeneracion-1900-1918/2da-epoca), accessed July 20, 2016.

because he wants the poor to remain, that is, to be the slaves of rich.[190]

In the same issue, Don Ricardo proclaimed in a framed announcement, *"Villarreal ya no es miembro de la Junta"* (Villarreal is no longer a member of the Junta). This little box became a standard feature in the paper for the next months.

The same issue contained an item, penned by Ethel Duffy Turner on the English page, headlined "Where are the guns?" The PLM conducted the abortive Baja Campaign at the time, and it seems that an American Sheriff, a man named Meadow, had crossed the international border under a Red Cross flag, ostensibly to aid *Fedérale* victims of a firefight. But when PLM fighters arrived on the scene, they discovered that the weapons of the victims were missing. According to Mrs. Turner, the Americans had stolen at least 12 rifles. The missing guns turned out to be critical, as Mrs. Turner recounted in her 1966 interview. Her husband spent much of his time during this period "looking for guns."[191]

The story also illustrates a major difference between the Flores Magón brothers and Madero: Madero came from money and Flores Magón did not. Camilo Arriaga, the man who paid for their flight into the United States, had authored the first *Partido Liberal Mexicana* program in 1900. As a financial supporter, he issued the PLM proclamation of 1906. Arriaga's reasons are unclear – whether he suffered from revolutionary jealousy because Flores Magón had usurped the role of revolutionary leader from him, or he was concerned with the new Junta's connection to extremists in the United States. Madero took the role of leading revolutionary chieftain from Flores Magón by 1911. In turn, Don Ricardo painted Madero as a member of the wealthy

---

[190] *Regeneración*, February 25, and various editions in March and April, 1911.
[191] Ibid.; Ethel Duffy Turner 1966 interview.

elite. *Regeneración* returned to this theme repeatedly. On April 15,1911, Don Ricardo wrote:

> *El Partido Maderista* represents the interests of the rich class because they care only about the fall of the tyrant Díaz, to recreate the vigor of the constitution of 1857; in a word to give the people political liberty. The people would then be free to vote, to have meetings, to show their thoughts (free to publish), but there would still be misery afoot because what law is there to abolish misery?[192]

Don Ricardo was certainly right about Don Francisco's origins. He came from money, and his family, while basically conservative, did support him financially. In 2012, historian Heribert von Feilitzsch tracked down money that the Mexican treasury under Secretary of Finance Ernesto Madero, Francisco's uncle, paid to the Madero's reimbursing their investment in the Revolution. The recipient was Gustavo Madero, the president's brother and one his closest advisors. The money was paid back in $50,000 increments (about $6.7 million in today's dollars). The expenses broke down as follows:

> $154,000 Arms, ammunition and equipment
> $ 53,000 Legal fees
> $ 6,000 confidential agency in New York
> $ 5,000 confidential agency in Washington
> $ 18,000 confidential agency in San Antonio
> $ 15,000 confidential agency in El Paso
> $ 56,000 Expeditions, envoys, trips and minor expenses.[193]

In verifying his information, von Feilitzsch noted that Sherburne G. Hopkins, a Washington-based lawyer and

---

[192] *Regeneración,* April 15, 1911.
[193] Von Feilitzsch, Heribert, *In Plain Sight: Felix A. Sommerfeld: Spymaster in Mexico, 1908 to 1914* (Amissville: Henselstone Verlag, 2012), pp. 100-101.

lobbyist, told a US Senate committee in 1920 that he knew the Madero family had invested $400,000 into the revolution. This is a country in which Díaz had written: "Thirty or forty thousand pesos, in my opinion, would be enough to change the face of the country."[194]

Madero was a reluctant revolutionary. He had backed into the fight, and his family forced him to curb both his tongue and his efforts until Díaz reacted in an overly paranoid fashion and forced the war upon him. Flores Magón had called for armed insurrection for many years, and was always certain that the time to act was at hand. Until 1910 he had been wrong. By the time, Mexico exploded with the rage that he helped to create, he was broke.

While Don Ricardo was perennially broke, he had other problems as well. He personally sponsored the revolt in Baja in both 1910 and 1911, but not only did they fall apart, the "insurgents" had few Mexicans among them. On May 10, 1911, *Maderista* forces under the command of Pascual Orozco disobeyed direct orders from Madero and took Ciudad Juarez. On May 21, representatives of the Díaz administration met with Madero in El Paso and signed the Treaty of Juarez.

The document dictated a provisional government, comprised mostly of *Porfirians*, that was to rule Mexico until elections could be held in October. Madero left for Mexico City, Díaz left for Europe, and a substantial number of American left-wing types journeyed to the Baja. The *Federales* (now part of the Madero presumptive government) easily defeated the white insurgents there to the general applause of the Mexican people and press. Very few of the "insurgents" were Mexican, and none of them

---

[194] Ibid, p. 404; Porfirio Díaz to José Yves Limantour, Sr., March 17, 1876, as quoted in Alfonso de María y Campos, "Porfirianos Prominentes: Origines y Anos de Juventud de Ocho Integrantes del Grupo de los Científicos, 1846-1876" (*Historia Mexicana*, Volume XXXIV, 4, April-June, 1985), p. 741.

were Mexican Indians. A researcher went into the area in 1962, and could not find a single indigenous individual that had stood with the insurgents, who were mostly white, Wobbly, and may have come for the promise of free land.[195]

The revolution in Baja had started against the troops of Díaz, but forces loyal to Madero defeated them in the end. And there were other breaks in the PLM lines. Shortly before the departure of Díaz, Filomeno Mata was released from Belen for the last time. He came out of his seven-month prison term, old and fatally ill, but made one last decision at *Diario del Hogar*. He named Juan Sarabía, one of the PLM Junta members that had fled to Canada in 1906, editor of the paper. Agents of Díaz had captured Sarabía in El Paso in 1907, hustled him across the border and imprisoned him at San Juan de Ulúa. One of the lawyers for the dissidents in that prison was Jesús Flores Magón.[196]

Like many other papers in Mexico, *Diario del Hogar* editorialized against the Baja "invasion," believing it was another attempt by powers in the United States to annex Mexican land. Sarabía had split with Don Ricardo, but they shared some beliefs, including the idea that the United States was a major threat to Mexican sovereignty.[197]

Madero still wanted to make peace with Don Ricardo and on June 13, 1910, he sent four men to negotiate with him. The first four included three of his closest associates: Antonio Villarreal (who had published *Regeneración* in St. Louis after the Flores Magón brothers had gone to Canada and then issued the Bogus *Regeneración* in Chihuahua), Sarabía, and Jesús, the older brother who had abandoned the struggle against Díaz in 1902 – all three of these men were now ardent *Maderistas*, and both Villarreal and

---

[195] Owen, Roger C. "Indians and Revolution: The 1911 Invasion of Baja," *California" Ethnohistory* 10, no. 4, pp. 373-395.
[196] Albro, Ward S., *Always a Rebel: Ricardo Flores Magón and the Mexican Revolution* (Fort Worth: Texas Christian University Press, 1992), p. 134.
[197] Mata, p. 89.

Sarabía had caught the editorial wrath of Don Ricardo. The fourth man was Abraham Gonzales, who served as the governor of Chihuahua under Madero and was later murdered on the orders of Victoriano Huerta. What was said at the meeting is unknown, but afterwards, Jesús complained bitterly, that his brothers were no longer brothers to him.[198]

The arrival of a fifth man became evident the next day, when Ricardo, Enrique, Librado Rivera and another staff member were arrested and charged with violation of the neutrality laws. That fifth man might well have been Felix Sommerfeld, who until the research of Heribert von Feilitzsch, was regarded as one of the shady characters that showed up in the Revolution.

He was a German naval intelligence agent, who later acted as an operative in the United States during World War I. He had joined the Madero campaign early in the spring of 1911, and became one of Madero's most trusted advisors and chief of the Mexican secret service. He was adept at keeping Madero's enemies in jail in the United States, and he – or somebody like him – master-minded the arrest. Three days later, the "PLM" forces in Baja reached an accord with *Maderista* emissaries. Despite "orders" from Don Ricardo, they laid down their weapons, got $10, were treated to lunch in a Chinese restaurant, and faded across the border from whence they had come.[199]

Don Ricardo made bail, probably with help of Emma Goldman, and spent the summer writing inflammatory editorials against his new enemies. Both the failure in Baja and his personal alignment with the American left caused him to lose credibility on the Mexican side of the border. John Turner left the paper, pushed in part, by Don Ricardo's vindictive attitude toward his old comrades.

---

[198] Lomnitz, p. 28.
[199] E-mail from Heribert von Feilitzsch, July, 2016; Lomnitz, p. 329.

On July 2, he published an editorial headlined, "Juan Sarabía – Judas." Sarabía republished the article in *Diario del Hogar*, and wrote an adjoining article explaining that he was not, nor had ever been, a *Maderista*. Then he and Villarreal published yet another bogus *Regeneración*, this time from Mexico City. Ricardo Flores *Magón* referred to the paper as *Degeneración*. But John Turner, too, turned away from him, attracting editorial wrath from *Regeneración*. The paper editorialized that Turner had gone over to the Madero side. William C. Owen, the new English page editor, published a letter demanding a retraction. It never happened.[200]

The 1911 case against the PLM took more than a year to get through court, and, in all probability, they were technically innocent. Ricardo Flores Magón received a lot of criticism in coming years for not crossing the border into Baja. There are a lot of arguments why he did not. Some people believed his companion, María Broussé, talked him out of it. Others pointed out that he was physically not fit enough for a military adventure: Although he was only 39 in 1910, it had been a hard 39 years. The fact of the matter is that he was simply not a soldier, and he knew that his strength was in his pen, not as an amateur soldier. He was also well aware of the law. As early as 1907, he had warned fellow revolutionaries about it:

> I have your last in your word of the squadron "Zaragoza", as I wrote you in my previous letter, you must not violate the laws of neutrality. I advise, therefore, that all the friends of revolutionary groups but only in Mexican Territory. Following that line of conduct, we will have nothing to fear from the aggression of the American Government in our matters.[201]

---

[200] *Regeneración*, July 2, 1910; Turner, pp. 261, 262.
[201] Ricardo Flores Magón to Calixto Guerra, August 7, 1907 (Archivos de Ricardo Flores Magón, http://archivomagon.net/obras-

Don Ricardo was not having a good year, and it kept getting worse. In August, the *Daily Call*, a leftist newspaper in New York, which had dismissed the PLM in Baja as "bandits," published an open letter from Juan Sarabía to Ricardo Flores Magón. In it he stated that Flores Magón revolution was unacceptable in Mexico, and that Mexicans were not ready for either socialism or anarchism. Undeterred, Don Ricardo issued a new PLM proclamation to replace the one of 1906. This time, his anarchist intents appeared very straightforward. In October, Mary Harris "Mother" Jones returned from Mexico and urged him to negotiate with Madero. His negative response caused her to label him a "fanatic."[202]

The day after his arrest on July 14, (the day after the visit from the *Maderistas*), 1911, *Regeneración* appeared with a two-page edition, one of them in English. The masthead on July 22 changed to read:

Semanal Revolucionario
Escrito por trabajadores y para los trabajadores
(Revolution weekly - Written by workers for the workers)[203]

William C. Owen, the new English page editor, gave the paper a strange disconnect. Owen, a British citizen, was a staunch anarchist. Several days after the arrest of the Flores Magón brothers and Anselmo L. Figueroa, he wrote about Don Ricardo making bail and referred to him as "Ricardo Magon" (indicating he did not even understand Hispanic names). He also ran a mini-biography of an English leftist, Tom Mann, and a letter to the editor, republished from an English newspaper. Items about left-wing groups in Chicago and New York began appearing on the English page. Since its first inception in 1900, *Regeneración* had been dedicated

completas/correspondencia-1899-1922/c-1907/cor258/), retrieved July 21, 2016.
[202] Bufe, Verter, pp. 360,361.
[203] *Regeneración,* July 22, 1911.

to the Mexican cause of ending Continuismo. Now, it embraced the broad range of left wing groups and a variety causes ranging from unionism to pacifism. The causes were so divergent to be divisive, and beyond the ken or care of many Mexican readers.[204]

From Mexico City, Villarreal wrote of his former comrade, that Ricardo Flores Magón was a "blackmailer, a swindler, a coward, a drunken pervert and scoundrel who shared his mistresses with all men of bad taste."[205]

The man who had replaced Don Ricardo as the head of the Mexican Revolution was about to run into his own problems. They would be exacerbated by a system he had not wanted to dismantle, and competing foreign interests – especially from the United States in the form of an American ambassador and the press.

Francisco Madero's popularity was indisputable – on October 1, in the only truly democratic presidential election in Mexican history up to then, he won 90 percent of the vote. However, a powerful coalition formed against him as a consequence. The *Porfiristas*, who had remained in power during the interim government of Francisco Leon de la Barra, did not go away. They allied with foreign interests led by a conniving US Ambassador to Mexico, Henry Lane Wilson, and, oddly enough, the press. Elected with Madero was José María Pino Suarez. The press - finally free to write - accused Pino Suarez of persecuting journalists in his native Yucatan where he served as interim governor in 1911; Still, Madero chose him as a running mate because of a political debt.

Pino Suarez had spent 80,000 pesos in 1909 on a daily newspaper espousing the *anti-reeleccionista* cause. But repayment of that carried a high price for Madero. Pino Suarez used existing laws against two newspapers in 1912

---

[204] Ibid, July 17, 1911.
[205] Bufe, Verter, p. 360.

and jailed a reporter after an unfavorable interview. These were the only transgressions against the press by the Madero administration, but they were enough. In January, Madero supporters complained bitterly to the president about the independent press. In turn, those journalists countered with articles defending the freedom of the press and articles on persecution of the press again became popular in Mexico City.[206]

Madero obviously recognized the importance of the press early in his political career and used it to his advantage. But the impressive array of pro-Madero newspapers created during the 1909 campaign was gone. Mata was dead, replaced by Sarabía, and Madero's only support in the press came from *Nueva Era*, a daily founded by his brother Gustavo, and *Diario Official*. During the Revolution, Madero had proclaimed that freedom of the press was "one of the most sacred principles..." When he came to power, he was beset by a series of revolts from both sides of the political spectrum. Newspapers frequently published grievances against him. He said in December 1912, "I don't read the press, and if I did, I would not believe the articles." He did, however, try to end the Díaz era subsidy system. Beyond ending blatant abuses, such as imprisonment of newspaper men (although that did not bother him on the other side of the border), Madero did little to change the laws concerning the press. Journalists charged that Madero's promise of a free press was hollow.[207]

Gustavo Madero, over his brother's objections, tried to control several of the larger dailies in Mexico City economically, but to no avail. Though Ernesto Madero, the president's uncle and Secretary of Finance, was nominally publisher of *El Imparcial,* the paper remained anti-Madero. The *Mexican Herald*, probably pushed by Ambassador

---

[206] Ugarte, Bravo, p. 82; Guzmán, *José María Pino Suarez*, p. 57; *El Correo de Chihuahua*, January 4, 1912.
[207] Taracena, p. 265.

Wilson, was also highly critical of the Maderos, and sent its critiques over the wires of the Associated Press. On several occasions, Madero interceded on behalf of journalists charged with defamation. When supporters urged him to control the press, he refused, saying "I prefer to sink with the law than to sustain myself without it." The length to which Madero carried freedom of the press, at least in Mexico City, now seems incredible. While Zapata was in open revolt against him in 1912, Madero personally approved the publication of Zapata's call for revolution in *Diario del Hogar*.[208]

If one reads the Mexican press during that period, or the reports generated by the *Mexican Herald* and disseminated through the Associated Press, Mexico was being torn apart. Ambassador Wilson's inaccurate reports to the US State Department also were misleading. Madero appeared to the American public a weak and ineffectual leader, and his image further suffered when the Mexican ambassador to the United States told a Chicago reporter in 1912 that fighting continued in Morelos and elsewhere. "The only way the government will be able to deal with these people," he said, "is to exterminate them."[209]

Regeneración published that statement, but by then the Flores Magón brothers served a 23-month sentence at MacNeil Island in Washington State. Ricardo Flores Magón was back in Mexico during the *Decena Trágica* (the ten tragic days, February 9-19, 1913), when his former nemesis was murdered by the joint hands of Victoriano Huerta and Henry Lane Wilson. Mexico was about to explode, but the Mexican Revolution had left Ricardo Flores Magón behind.

---

[208] Ross, pp. 233-235; Calvert, p. 114.
[209] *El Imparcial*, January 1 through 30, 1-30, 1913; *Mexican Herald*, January 1-30, 1913; Ethel Duffy Turner, p. 288.

Chapter 12

"A better class of men..."

Madero ruled Mexico for 14 tumultuous months. General Victoriano Huerta usurped his presidency and in turn faced the armies of Álvaro Obregón, Eulalio Gutiérrez, Emiliano Zapata and Pancho Villa, for a time all organized under the banner of Venustiano Carranza's Constitutionalist forces. Later in the civil war, the combined forces of Villa and Zapata occupied Mexico City, though in the end they relinquished the capital to Obregón. Zapata was murdered in 1919, when Obregón seized power from then-president Carranza, who in turn was murdered in 1920. Villa died in a hail of assassin's bullets in 1923, and Obregón was murdered in 1928. Through the violent phase of the Revolution, 1914 to 1920, there were multiple indigenous uprisings, always aiming to reclaim the land they wanted to till communally.

Although Ricardo Flores Magón editorially opposed each successive administration, when he was not in prison, until his own death in Leavenworth Penitentiary in November 1922, his impact was negligible. The power of his words had not decreased, but the impact and number of his supporters in Mexico had.

Madero and all the regimes that followed his had to deal with flare-ups of indigenous people demanding *Tierra y Libertad*, and each regime made some promises. When the Carranza administration created the Constitution of 1917, it appeared to be a win-win situation. Under Article three, the rights of all

Mexicans were restored; Article Seven guaranteed the freedom of speech and the press, and Article Twenty-Seven gave the government the right to all land and was tasked to promote land and wealth distribution.[210]

But there were problems. The first, of course, is that laws, even constitutions, are paper and need force to enforce them. Mexican journalists certainly had learned that the original Article 7 in the 1857 Constitution, the guarantee of freedom of the press, did little to protect them. The Lerdo laws of the reform, supposedly created to ensure equitable distribution of land (mostly away from the Catholic Church) had led to the land grabs during the *Porfiriato*. Ricardo Flores Magón objected to the inclusion Article 27 because of its opening:

> Article 27. Ownership of the lands and waters within the boundaries of the national territory is vested originally in the Nation, which has had, and has, the right to transmit title thereof to private persons, thereby constituting private property.[211]

When Ricardo Flores Magón emerged from the Arizona prison in 1910, he had given up all pretense of being an anarchist in disguise. In March 1911, he made clear one his major differences with Madero concerning the "right of property:"

> The right of property is ancient, as ancient as man's stupidity and blindness; but just the antiquity of a right cannot give it the "right" to survive. If it is an absurd right, it is necessary to abolish it without giving importance to its birth at the time when man covered his nakedness with the animal skins… The right of property is an absurd right because it had its

---

[210] *Mexican Constitutions 1857-1917*, translated by H. N. Branch in Jstor (https://archive.org/stream/jstor-1013370/1013370_djvu.txt), retrieved July 28, 2016.

[211] Ibid.

origins in crime, fraud, and abuse of power. In the beginning, the individual's right of territorial property did not exist. Land was worked in common, forests provided firewood to the hearths of all, harvests were distributed among the members of the community according to their needs. Examples of this nature can still be seen in some primitive tribes, and even in Mexico this custom thrived in indigenous communities in the era of Spanish domination, and lived until relatively recently, being the attempted act of despotism to take away the lands of those indigenous tribes...[212]

Writing in 1969, historian Eric R. Wolf divided the belligerents of the Mexican Revolution into three types: The "Centralist" represented the ideals of the *Porfiriato* regime, best exemplified by Victoriano Huerta. This faction believed that only a "strong man" could rule Mexico. Many foreign interests, including US Ambassador Henry Lane Wilson and the British government, which recognized the Huerta government (The US government did not) certainly agreed with that notion. In a 1917 biography, British writer David Hannay explained the reasons that drove Díaz from office as the "Indian Problem." The problem was, he wrote, that the majority of Mexicans were:

Mestizo, not only in blood but in thinking... How are you to persuade men, who do not value what civilized Europeans or citizens of the United States consider indispensable things, to work in order to gain them as Europeans will, and to desire what he desires?[213]

---

[212] as translated by Bufe, p. 375.
[213] Wolf, Eric R., *Peasant Wars of the 20th Century* (New York: Harper books, 1969), pp. 26, 27.

Hannay would brook no criticism of Díaz. As for Indians, "There is nothing to be done with such human beings... but suppress them."

Wolf identified the second group of belligerents as the liberals, but identifies that group with the ideals put forth in the late 19th and early 20th century, best represented by Madero, then Carranza and then Obregón. He did not include the PLM of Ricardo Flores Magón. The historian discounted the advances of both Villa from the North (an army seemingly comprised mostly of *Vaqueros*) and Zapata from the South (comprised mostly of *Indios*) because neither man had the ability nor desire to run the country. Their basic impact, Wolf claimed, was to force the subsequent regimes of both Carranza and Obregón to at least pay lip service to the idea of social reforms.[214]

The third group of belligerents, Wolf wrote, were the indigenous people, anarchists, basically the "rabble of the Revolution" that provided the personnel for all the armies involved. He linked these people, logically, to the new PLM. Some were indeed PLM members, but for the most part, they weren't. Ricardo Flores Magón had lost so much credibility in the Baja campaigns of 1911 and had alienated so many of his longtime allies by his sharp turn to the left that his influence had vanished.

By the time of his imprisonment in 1912, Ricardo Flores Magón was marginalized. Lomnitz points out that Don Ricardo was not censured as much as before in the various jails and prisons that housed him because neither the Mexican nor the US governments considered him a force in the Mexican situation. He had broken with the most famous American writer involved, John Kenneth Turner, and he had alienated the most influential Mexican intellectuals of the Revolution.[215]

---

[214] Wolf, p. 39, 40, 41.
[215] Lomnitz, p. 427.

Ricardo Flores Magón was still a fine and persuasive writer, but the men who controlled (as best they could) the fate of the Mexican Revolution could not accept what he was writing. These men, even those who had stood with him after his 1903 departure, were Mestizos, and most of them, especially leaders like Carranza and Obregón, had ambitions but lacked the good intentions of Francisco I. Madero. If they read Don Ricardo at all, what they read probably infuriated them.

June 15, 1912, on leaders, Ricardo Flores Magón wrote:

> The masses have the firm belief that it is necessary to have a leader or a man on a white horse at their head, that he'll conduct them toward their destiny, that he will carry them to tyranny or liberty; the question is whether he lead them with kindness or by spitting on them toward the good or the bad... Let each one of you be your own leader...[216]

On March 12, 1912, ten months after Porfirio Díaz had abdicated and Madero's popularity was at a high point in Mexico, he wrote:

> Porfirio Díaz and Francisco Madero feel in these moments the need to unite, in their own turn, with the popular masses. The first of these has been a savage beast who has sustained his dominion by cutting the throats of the Mexican Race; the second has been an evil *hacendado*...[217]

Strong words, indeed. During the Baja campaigns, the circulation of *Regeneración* and its revenues increased substantially, but much of that, like the soldiers who fought in those campaigns, came from north of the border. Although Ricardo Flores Magón had become a poster child for the American left, his direct impact on affairs in Mexico –

---

[216] Ricardo Flores Magón, writing in *Regeneración*, as translated by Bufe, pp. 248-249.
[217] Ibid, p. 254.

in terms of political clout with the people who were making decisions, was insubstantial. The newspaper he was running, basically without advertising, still printed photographs (an expensive process in those days) and his English page editor, William C. Owen, carried "news items" that addressed the left wing in America as much as the situation in Mexico - an article announcing a socialist fund in Chicago raiser would appear next to a situation report from a Mexican state. In October of 1913, after Don Ricardo served out a prison term in McNeil Island in Washington State, Owen, the man who had told him that the *campesinos* of Mexico did not have the education to differentiate between socialism, communism or anarchy, wrote and complained the paper was falling apart financially. During the last five years of the publication, 1913-1918, personal pleas for money for signed by Don Ricardo, were commonplace in the paper.[218]

But those vying for power in Mexico had not completely forgotten him. President Woodrow Wilson decided in 1915 to recognize a faction in Mexico as the legitimate government. He had a choice between Venustiano Carranza and candidates put forth by Pancho Villa, who commanded the by then greatly diminished División del Norte.

Carranza wanted it badly enough to set up a ruse. In the summer of 1915, Mexicans and Mexican-Americans in the American Southwest rose in revolt with the aim to reclaim the territory lost to the United States during the Mexican-American War of 1848. In their book, *The Plan de San Diego: Tejano Rebellion, Mexican Intrigue*, historians Charles Harris and Louis Sadler, demonstrate that Carranza created and financed the so-called Plan de San Diego to pressure the US government toward recognizing him as

---

[218] Lomnitz, p. 16; review of *Regeneración*, various editions in 1913-1918, accessed from *The Anarchist Annals of Ricardo Flores Magón*, (http://archivomagon.net/periodicos/regeneracion-1900-1918/2da-epoca), accessed July, 2016.

president as the only viable force to control the 'threat."
Carranza was easily able to thrust the responsibility on the
Magonistas. And Harris and Sadler correctly noted:

> The *Plan de San Diego* has the same grandiose
> unreality as some of the other *Magonista* schemes,
> and given that faction's impressive record of military
> incompetence, it had absolutely no chance for
> success.[219]

In response to the accusations, Carranza agents had
planted and published in US newspapers, Ricardo Flores
Magón played directly into the hands of the Carranza
conspirators. In a series of editorials, on October 2, October
9 and October 30, 1915, he correctly pointed out that
Carranza had fabricated the rumors about his involvement
in this movement, although he misinterpreted the motives
as a means for the Carranza faction to get him into legal
trouble with the US government. In the past, he had written
several moving articles about the injustices of the Texas
legal system that often left claimants as victims of lynching.
On October 30, he went too far and called all Mexican to
arms, and to prove that he and his followers were not
bandits, he noted that:

> We will not lay down our arms until the following four
> goals are attained:

> 1. Abolition of all government of man by man.
> 2. Elimination of capitalist.
> 3. Extermination of Clericalism.
> 4. That the land become the common property of the
>   producers of social wealth.[220]

Idealism among revolutionary leadership, except for Zapata,
who was murdered later, died with Madero. Carranza had
worked a deal with the unions, and made promises of land

---

[219] Harris, Sadler, *The Plan de San Diego*, p. 23.
[220] *Regeneración*, October 2,9 and 30, 1915, as translated by Bufe, pp.
202-206.

reform. In a choice between Carranza and Villa, President Wilson could be expected to naturally gravitate toward the individual who was more like him, therefore not the semi-literate (at best) Villa. But Carranza pushed it further by making it clear that the Plan de San Diego was written in anarchist terms, and he complained to the US government and the US Post Office that *Regeneración* was causing the problems along the border by urging violence among Mexicans and Mexican-Americans. On February 18, 1916, American law enforcement officials arrested the Flores Magón brothers for sending materials through the mail that incited "murder, arson and treason." The officers beat Enrique so badly that he had to be taken to a hospital before jail. William C. Owen, faced indictment but fled to England.[221]

By the time of the trial, Don Ricardo was so ill that he could not attend it. He was sentenced to a year; Enrique to three years, and Don Ricardo was released pending appeal. The American left had raised the bail. On several occasions in the past, the US Postal Service revoked the paper's second class mailing permit. Now it happened again. Further, Ricardo Flores Magón aligned himself so closely with the anarchist cause that he lost support even among the socialists, communists and the labor movement. Throughout their American odyssey, the underlining theme was poverty. *Regeneración*'s English page editor, William C. Owen was indicted, but successfully fled the country to return to his native England. After Owen's departure, the subtitle on the masthead "by the workers and for the workers" disappeared, and for the last two years of the paper's existence, calls for contributions for the editors' legal defense were commonplace in the paper.[222]

A growing rift developed between Enrique and Ricardo. In December 1916, Enrique traveled to San Francisco and

---

[221] Bufe, Verter, pp. 80, 81, 366.
[222] Ibid; various editions of *Regeneración* in 1916,1917,1918.

delivered a speech to a large group of "radicals," both in English and in Spanish. The brothers were still fighting their 1916 conviction. They published an article explaining, "there is no hope in the appellate court" so the case had to be brought to the Supreme Court. Unfortunately, that would cost $500, and there was only $100 in the defense fund. On October 17, 1917, Enrique appeared on the masthead as editor for the last time. The 1916 conviction sent him to prison, and the legal strategy used against Don Ricardo was about to change.[223]

So far, legal attacks against *Regeneración* had come in three different guises: first were libel suits filed in Mexico; second, on occasion the post master, for various reasons, revoked their second class mailing permit (this is economically devastating to any print publication and it happened to *Regeneración* in St Louis and twice in Los Angeles), and finally the Flores Magón brothers were accused of violating the US neutrality laws on two occasions. As the World War progressed and the United States slid closer to joining the war, times and laws were changing. Don Ricardo seemed unaware of the currents he was now swimming against.

On March 17, 1917, he wrote a glowing report on the Russian Revolution, which the paper published on its English page. On April 21, he wrote an article on "world revolution."[224] The United States was now at war with Germany, and many Americans, particularly well-to-do and well-connected Americans, moved into the kind of thinking that eventually generated the "Red Scare" of the early 1920s.

---

[223] Verter and Bufe described the split as a "family Squabble" (p. 367). Lomnitz contends that Enrique was beginning to see himself as the natural heir to Don Ricardo (p. 468); *Regeneración*, December 9, 1917, October 17, 1917.
[224] *Regeneración*, April 21 and March 17, 1917.

The last issue of *Regeneración* appeared on March 16,1918. It contained only two pages, (they forgot to change the "English Section Page four" box on the masthead), and the English section (on page 2) featured a single letter from the now imprisoned and soon to be deported Emma Goldman. The front page also contained a Manifesto printed in Spanish to "the Anarchists of the World and to Workers of the World in General." Six days later, law enforcement agents arrested Don Ricardo and Librado Rivera for sedition under the new Espionage Act, passed just weeks before. In August, Don Ricardo was sentenced to 20 years at MacNeil Island. Later he transferred to Fort Leavenworth for medical reasons. Rivera received 15 years in a penitentiary. Enrique lost his appeal and ended up in Leavenworth for three years.

One would assume the story is over. But not quite.

Chapter 13

Men in Suits

In June 1918, federal officers apprehended and interrogated Felix A. Sommerfeld in New York City for three days. They knew little about the man, except that he had come to the United States in the early part of the century, had sought his luck in mining in northern Mexico, and had been involved in the Madero government, after which time he had ties to both the Carranza government and Pancho Villa.

"I have a long and convenient memory," he mused as he calmly answered all their questions for three days, save one. When asked which side in the present conflict between Germany and the United States his sentiments were on, he simply said, "I will not answer that question."

His memory was more convenient than long. They learned that he had been a security man for President Francisco Madero, a man he admired, and later represented Pancho Villa in the US. He also bought munitions for the revolutionary chieftain when it was legal. But when the conflict arose between the Carranza and Villa factions and threatened to spill over into the United States in 1915, he claimed to have retired from Mexican affairs. They did not know that he was a member of Germany's notorious "Secret War Council" in New York that wreaked havoc on American labor relations, manufacturing and shipping during the

World War. He had been a German secret agent on this continent since 1908.[225]

Unlike Ricardo Flores Magón, whose photos appeared on PLM promissory note, adjacent to newspaper stories and almost every PLM poster or graphic designs created for left wing magazines, Sommerfeld was a man in the shadows. He was responsible for the shipment of millions of dollars' worth of ammunition into Mexico during the Revolution, may well have instigated Pancho Villa's Columbus Raid in 1916, and was part of a German team that wreaked havoc in the United States with bombings. He was directly responsible for at attempt to divert American munitions away from the front lines. But to his interrogators, he was just a German national, living well in the United States. Beyond that, he was well connected – he knew many people in the US government and lived in a nice hotel. Most importantly, he was not a "red" or an "anarchist."

He was interned at a camp in Fort Oglethorpe, Georgia, as an "enemy alien" (not a spy) until the end of the war, and then, for all practical purposes, disappeared.[226]

---

[225] See von Feilitzsch, Heribert, *The Secret War Council: The German Fight Against the Entente in America in 1914* (Amissville: Henselstone Verlag, 2015); also von Feilitzsch, Heribert, *The Secret War on the United States: A Tale of Sabotage, Labor Unrest and Border Troubles* (Amissville: Henselstone Verlag, 1915).

[226] Some of the above is drawn from the June, 1918 interview, but the overview of the life and activities of Felix Sommerfeld is drawn from the work of von Feilitzsch, Heribert, *In Plain Sight: Felix A. Sommerfeld, Spymaster in Mexico, 1908-1914* (Amissville: Henselstone Verlag, 2012); *Felix Sommerfeld and the Mexican Front in the Great War* (Amissville: Henselstone Verlag, 2014).

Chapter 14

The Long Goodbye

On August 15, 1917, a US federal court convicted Ricardo Flores Magón and Librado Rivera under the Espionage Act, received 20 and 15 years respectively, and taken to MacNeil Island to begin serving their sentences. Don Ricardo was limited to writing three letters a week, no more than two pages in length. In December, he wrote an old comrade, Gus Teltsch that he was being transferred to Leavenworth because of his health. Librado transferred with him and spent much of the next three years in the cell adjacent to Don Ricardo. Enrique, convicted under the US neutrality laws, also came to Leavenworth.[227]

In the summer of 1920, Don Ricardo began a long correspondence with Henry Weinberg, a New York attorney who stayed in contact with him until the very end. In his third letter to Weinberg, he discussed his health, his history and the philosophy that had led him to prison, and did so in a manner that reflected his early legal training:

> Now, my dear Mr. Weinberger, I am going to state the facts in my case, but it is not with the purpose of my asking for clemency, for I will never ask for such a thing. It is for you and my friends to know why I am

---

[227] Ricardo Flores Magón to Gus Teltsch, December 19, 1920. Digital Archives of Ricardo Flores Magón (http://archivomagon.net/obras-completas/correspondencia-1899-1922/c-1920/cor10-2/), accessed August 1, 2016.

in prison. You and they will seek the best way to get me out of prison, without my having to humiliate myself asking for clemency.

I shall be forty-six years old on the 16th of this coming September; Mexican; married, and having two children. In the Department of Justice must be a report on file made on the last months of 1918 by the doctor of the Penitentiary of McNeil Island, wherein it is stated that I am afflicted with diabetes and rheumatism, being this the reason why I was transferred to this institution. In addition to this, I am going blind.

Enrique will be released on the 10th of next September, having by then his term expired. But Librado Rivera will remain here, who as you will see in the indictment, was charged with me of having violated the Espionage Act. Please ask Mr. J. H. Ryckman, Higgins Bldg., Los Angeles, Cal. for a copy of the indictment, and all legal data. Mr. Ryckman was one of my lawyers. I do not write him asking for the papers, because I have already written the number of letters I am entitled each week.

I was the editor of *Regeneración*, a Spanish newspaper published in Los Angeles, Cal., and Librado was one of my associates. In the issue of March 16th, 1918, I published an appeal to the workers of all countries; appeal which was signed by Rivera and myself.

The appeal of the manifesto had as its purpose to acquaint the workers of the world with the conditions prevailing at the time all over the world. It was an exposition of these facts: The European war was a source of discontent and unrest among the masses of all countries, that this unrest was made evident by riots, strikes, and several others acts of protest taking place all over the world. Riots, strikes and acts of protest that will eventually culminate in a world-wide revolution, that revolution involves chaos, as it is the blind effort of the masses to free themselves from intolerable conditions, and chaos offers to the unscrupulous, the charlatan, and the knave the most brilliant opportunity of enriching themselves, and of establishing a crueler tyranny than the one destroyed; that, however, the world-wide revolution was inevitable; that no one could stop or prevent it, for revolutions are social phenomena which are begotten by causes that lie out of the control of the individual, like the storm, the cyclone, the eruption of a volcano are natural phenomena which one can predict, but not to prevent; and being it so that we workers were impotent to prevent the impending worldwide revolution, our duty were to avoid the ensuing chaos, to which end we should prepare the mentality of the masses propagating the anarchist ideals of universal brotherhood and peace based on justice.

The foregoing is the essence of the manifesto or appeal. No one incitation to violence was made. I wrote the manifesto, and I had not in my mind the idea of making a revolution, but of counteracting the evils inherent to all popular upheavals. Even less was in my mind the idea of overthrowing the United States government. I thought in conditions of the world at large, without having in my mind one particular country.

Nobody dares to prosecute the man who announces the coming of a storm, the eruption of a volcano, the toppling over an avalanche. On the contrary his prediction is seriously taken, and is considered useful, for by its means humanity is able to avoid, or, at least, to lessen the ravages of the catastrophe. However, Librado Rivera and myself were arrested

155

on the 21st of March, 1918, and charged with violation of the Espionage Act, tried and sentenced.[228]

Oddly, his correspondence with his wife/lover/companion was sparse in the archives covering his last prison sentence. He made it clear if deported, he wanted time to arrange to take her and her daughter with him. He made references to Maria in both his letters to his lawyer and to Ellen White, a woman he developed an intimate correspondence with. She was also known as "Lilly Saroff" and Don Ricardo often seemed to send messages to other old comrades using their code names when both the United States government and the agency working for Díaz hunted him. But while his letters to Weinberger reflected his knowledge of the process of law, he let loose his literary side when corresponding to Ms. White:

My weapon -my pen- the only weapon I have ever wielded; the weapon that landed me here; the weapon that accompanied me through the infernos of a thirty years' struggle for what is beautiful, will be then as useless as a broken sword in the hands of a warrior beset with enemies, and I shall toss it at the face of Darkness besetting me... Yes, by then my pen will be absolutely useless. A bird may brush past, but my pen will be impotent to depict the graceful flight; the stars will continue piercing the dark flesh of the Night with their cold glimmer, but my idle pen, insensible to Beauty, will not even reflect in its rusty surface a single ray of their heavenly light. Do you understand, my good comrade, how my poor pen will become an encumbrance, a nuisance, the

---

[228] Ricardo Flores Magón to Henry Weinberger, August 5, 1920, Digital Archives of Ricardo Flores Magón (http://archivomagon.net/obras-completas/correspondencia-1899-1922/c-1920/cor10-2/), accessed August 1, 2016.

most useless of all things? A rock contributes to the charms of a landscape; the old, dead trunk renders to Beauty an invaluable service by suffering the ivy to display on it its exquisite tracery, but what is an idle pen good for? Can it, perhaps, translate into iridescent words the light that plays on a feminine curve? Or, could it ever gather in the virginal whiteness of a sheet of paper, so as to render them precise, and clear, and vivid, the indefinite, vague, colorless, yet only too real, because too pungent, longings of all the unfortunates who breathe on Earth?[229]

It was not a good time to be an anarchist in the United States. There were a series of strikes that summer, and on June 2, 1919, seven bombs went off in seven major cities, including New York and Washington, and the homes of a New York judge and the attorney general of the United States were damaged. At each bomb site, there were pink fliers that read: "There will be bloodshed. We will do anything and everything to supres(sic) the capitalist class."[230]

Don Ricardo knew no help was coming from Mexico. After ten years of violence, which saw at least a million die and another million Mexican immigrate, the country at last seemed stable. Alvaro Obregón had outgoing president Venustiano Carranza murdered because he knew Carranza believed in civilian, not military rule. After the short interim presidency of Adolfo de la Huerta, Obregón was "elected" president in December. He gave certain concessions to

---

[229] Henry Weinberger to Ricardo Flores Magón, November 18,1922; Ricardo Flores Magón to Ellen White, December 27,1921, http://archivomagon.net/obras-completas/correspondencia-1899-1922/c-1921/cor87-2, accessed August 1, 2016.

[230] Gage, Beverly, *The Day Wall Street exploded: A History of the American in its first Age of Terror* (New York-London: Oxford University Press, 2009), p. 27.

unions and made deals with American oil companies, and this led to the recognition of his government by the US Government. He had to handle a minor revolt by de la Huerta, but the country was stable, and Obregón, stepped down, just as Porfirio Díaz had stepped down in 1880. Obregón wanted Plutarco Elías Calles to be his Manuel Gonzales (who fronted for Díaz from 1881 to 1884), and he was duly elected again in 1928, but was assassinated before re-assuming the office. Together, Obregón and Calles (who would become the *Jefe Politico* – Political Boss - of Mexico until Lázaro Cárdenas kicked him out of the country in 1934) formed the basis of the *Partido Revolucionario Institucional* (the Party of the Institutionalized Revolution). These men believed in the Porfirian strategy for governing Mexico. Historian Enrique Krauze outlined the 12 steps of Porfirian rule in 1987:

1. Repression or pacification
2. Divide and Conquer
3. Control and flexibility in government
4. Ineffective suffrage – re-election
5. Control of legislative power
6. Control of Judicial Power
7. *Pan o Palo* (Bread or stick)
8. Political reconciliation with the Church
9. Creating the image of "Statesmanship" outside of Mexico
10. Control of the press
11. Control of intellectuals
12. Development of a personal following.[231]

Both Obregón and Calles knew who Ricardo Flores Magón was and they did not want him back, at least not alive. They knew that northern Mexico had always been a hot bed of

---

[231] Krauze, Enrique, *Porfirio Díaz, Místico de la Autoridad* (México: Fondo de la Cultura, 1987), pp. 31-32.

revolution, and they also knew why. Writing in 1961, Michael C. Meyer noted:

> In the first decade of the 20th century, Chihuahua possessed a relatively large middle class of merchants, artisans, coachmen, railroad men and clerks. There is some evidence to suggest that these middle groups maintained a limited contact with their social counter parts in the United States and, in emulation of the better defined middle sector north of the Rio Grande, desired to better their lot. As a result, the middle groups within the state were susceptible to the endless stream of revolutionary propaganda that saturated Chihuahua during the last few years of the Díaz dictatorship.[232]

And who would that be except the Flores Magón brothers – first all three of them from 1901 to 1903, and then Enrique and Ricardo from 1904 to 1907. Ricardo and Enrique were in prison from 1907 to 1910, and when they came out, they moved so far to the left that the supporters mentioned above abandoned them. Don Ricardo made the constant mistake of believing the pot he was stirring was ready to boil over, and then refused, in 1911, to accept partial victory when Madero reached out to him.

Don Ricardo remained a true believer until the very end, but his letters reveal both deteriorating health and misplaced hope of release. He wrote in April 1922 to Alice Stone Blackwell:

> I cough a great deal, and a pain in the inside at the level of the heart is always present. I was so sick last February that for two weeks I spit blood when coughing. My eyesight, on the other hand, is constantly growing dimmer as a result of the cataracts I have in both eyes, and I can only read or write by means of a powerful reading glass. As

---

[232] Meyer, Sherman, *The Course of Mexican History,* p. 9.

though I had not already enough trouble, my kidneys ache, and this makes me suspect that the diabetes I was suffering when I was received in McNeil Island in 1918 to begin the term has not disappeared. Such is the state of my health, yet the Department of Justice assures my friends that my physical condition is good, when in its files must be the report sent by the physician at McNeil Island in 1918, certifying that I was suffering from diabetes and rheumatism, and the report sent by the physician of this institution (Leavenworth) in 1920, telling that I had cataracts in both eyes, and anemia. The existence of the cataracts was confirmed by a private expert that my friends sent in to examine my eyes, early in 1921. Diabetes is considered an incurable disease, or at least as one hard to be cured - it is possible that this malady might have disappeared when I have not gotten the special diet recommended for its treatment? And as for the cataracts, are they not a breach in the health of a person, that one may consider the health of him who suffers from them as good? Now, without being a physician, no one can say that a person, who continually coughs, has a dull constant pain in his left side which may be symptom of a decaying lung, and has expectorated blood for two weeks, may be in good health. Perhaps I am not already a consumptive, but I my condition of life do not change and if do not move to a more congenial climate, tuberculosis will certainly be the outcome of these, for me, alarming symptoms. Of the laboratory analysis of the sputum the official voice is silent. Why? A sample of sputum was asked of me last February. I gave it, and was told as there were no experts here to make its analysis, it was to be sent with that purpose to the laboratory at Topeka,

Kansas, which must be that of the State Bureau of Health.[233]

In the last year of his life, Ricardo Flores Magón developed a poetic melancholy that stayed with him until the end. On December 27, 1921, he wrote to Ellen White after some 24 political prisoners had been released that Christmas. He complained that the few people who served sentences as long as his were overlooked, and then he looked back on his work with a writer's regret and pride. Ten days before his death, still hoping for deportation, he again wrote Ellen White,

> I am glad you will not insist in depicting you so differently from the way... of you and I thank you for allowing me to say that you are nice.
>
> Yes, I am sorry, too, that we shall never meet again... But if I go free soon, I hope to be able of bidding you good-bye, my beloved comrade.
>
> I should close this letter now. Yes, it is cold, and I dream of the south, and its sky, and its flowers. Before long, perhaps, shall I be blessed with its beauty... And when by my native cliffs, I happen to discern the vague outline of the northern shores on which lay scattered the wreckage of so many hopes of mine, I shall say with a sigh - I meant well, my blonde brothers, I meant well, but you could not understand me...[234]

---

[233] Ricardo Flores Magón to Alice Stone Blackwell, April 11, 1922 (http://archivomagon.net/obras-completas/correspondencia-1899-1922/c-1921/cor87-2/), accessed August 1, 2016.

[234] Ricardo Flores Magón to Ellen White, November 12. 1922 (http://archivomagon.net/obras-completas/correspondencia-1899-1922/c-1921/cor87-2/), accessed October 3, 2016.

Ricardo and Enrique Flores Magón in a Los Angeles Jail ca. 1917.
Creative Commons.

Still, he remained true to his cause and resigned to this fate. He wrote in an earlier letter:

You blame the workers, my good, generous comrades, for be so indifferent as not to place their vigorous arms between me and my executioners, but are they really to be blamed for my fate? No, they are innocent. They did not appoint me their champion to fight their battles for them - I appointed myself. I saw them being so ugly, and so ignorant, and so weak under the weight of their chains that my beauty-loving soul was shocked, and it was thus that I become a rebel. It is all my fault, the sin of my nerves to get jarred at the sight of injustice, the crime of my heart always craving for beauty. I wanted the ugly masses to be beautiful by the only means of getting so - Freedom! - and being too small for so gigantic an enterprise, I failed, alas! But my dream of beauty is worth any sacrifice.[235]

Four days before his death, he received good news from Henry Weinberger, who informed him that the deportation hearings in his case had been completed. Warrants would be issued for deportation, and the Pardon Attorney was going to make a report to the Attorney General. "I hope in hopes for early good news for you."

Ricardo Flores Magón was found dead in his cell the morning of November 21, 1922. But his story was far from over. As so often happens after the death of a creative person, everybody seemed to want a part of him. The government wanted him back as a hero, but Obregón had yet to make the deals with the US oil companies. Enrique had been released from Leavenworth in 1921 and lived in Los Angeles. He rejected the idea of government sponsorship that would provide the $740 to bring his brother home. Antonio Díaz Soto y Gama, an intellectual who had been aligned with Zapata during the Revolution, gave a stirring eulogy for Don Ricardo the day after his death, but both Enrique and Maria Broussé, Don Ricardo's common law wife, refused his help to bring the body home, and both agreed he should not be buried in the United States.

Unfortunately, by the time his body arrived in Los Angeles, it was decomposing badly. Supporters raised the money for embalming, but there were too many people in Los Angeles who had been close to the brothers, that a proper funeral seemed necessary. It would be the first of three. He was temporarily buried, dug up and transported to Mexico City

---

[235] Henry Weinberger to Ricardo Flores Magón, November 18,1922; Ricardo Flores Magón to Ellen White, December 27,1921, http://archivomagon.net/obras-completas/correspondencia-1899-1922/c-1921/cor87-2, accessed August 1, 2016.

on January 15, where again he was interred in a private cemetery. Years later, he find his final resting place in the *Rotunda de los Hombres Ilustres.*[236]

But the fighting over Ricardo Flores Magón legacy continued. María and Enrique both staked out claims to be his intellectual and revolutionary heirs and the anarchists of the world united behind their "martyr." Of course, "martyrs" have to be murdered, so the story spread quickly that he had actually been beaten to death. Most internet searches of Ricardo Flores Magón will inform the reader that he was beaten to death in his cell. Lomnitz doesn't wholeheartedly agree, but Bufe and Verter support the idea completely. Researcher Andrew Grant Wood went back and examined both, available correspondence from his time and at MacNeil Island and Leavenworth, and concluded that Don Ricardo had died on "not so benign medical neglect." His medical problems were largely incurable, but treatable and if he had been transferred to a public hospital, proper treatment would have improved and prolonged his life.[237]

Ricardo Flores Magón is basically unknown in the United States today. In Mexico, according to Lomnitz, school children are taught about the Flores Magón brothers, but have trouble distinguishing between Jesús, Enrique and Ricardo. In both countries, as we have seen, historians disregard him for a variety of cultural and political reasons. Anarchists, of course, know and love him. *Dreams of Freedom: A Ricardo Flores Magón Reader*, edited by Chaz Bufe and Mitchell Cowen Verter, is, by its own admission, the largest collection of translated material written by Don Ricardo. It contains 52 articles and stories from his pen, mostly translated by Mr. Bufe, but only 11 of those were

[236] Lomnitz, pp. 494-502.
[237] Ibid; Wood, Andrew Grant, "Death of a political Prisoner: Revisiting the case of Ricardo Flores Magón" (Oklahoma: University of Tulsa Press, *A Contracorriente Magazine*, no date), accessed at https://www.ncsu.edu/project/acontracorriente/fall_05/Wood.pdf, retrieved July 20, 2016.

from before 1910, the year Ricardo Flores Magón decided to go public with his anarchist beliefs.

The matches the Flores Magón brothers lit and threw into the tinderbox of Mexico consisted of the articles in the original *Regeneración* in Mexico City in 1900 and 1901, in *El Hijo de Ahuizote* in 1902, and the reborn *Regeneración* in 1904, the point at which the two brothers fled to Canada and issued the PLM manifesto.

"The history of Mexican journalists," Rafael Loret de Mola wrote in 1987, "is the history of the struggle between liberty and power." Arguably, that is the struggle of journalism everywhere. It could also be argued that is also the struggle of historians. In the re-examination of the life and times of Ricardo Flores Magón, the indication is that both struggles, those of journalists and those of historians, are in danger of being lost.[238]

---

[238] Loret de Mola, Rafael, *Denuncia*, (México: Grijalbo, 1987), pp.237-238.

Conclusion

I must admit that bad beer in Texas led me to Mexico and almost got me killed. I was in El Paso at a hotel, intending to take bus to Ciudad de Chihuahua the next morning where I had arranged an interview with Margarita Terrazas, the daughter of Silvestre Terrazas. I went down to the hotel bar to have a beer.

This was 1986. In those days throughout the Midwest and extending down into Texas, breweries would deliver their beer in refrigerated trucks. This was long before mini-breweries. A beer was a beer even after you had a Hamm's. And if that beer had been cold and had gotten warm because it was stored outside a cooler, you got an awful tasting beer - but then again, since prohibition, Americans got used to drinking bad beer.

I had one - very bad - and then decided to jump on one of the little red buses that took tourists across the river into Ciudad Juarez.

Mexico is justly known for its beer, because around 1900, Porfirio Díaz had decided people were drinking too much pulque, so he sent a delegation to Germany to hire as many of the best brew masters they could - they came back and started producing excellent beer - much of which is still available to this day.

So, I wandered from cervezeria to cervezeria, sampling wares and practicing my bad Spanish. I was 39 years old and had been a working journalist - at least writing for publication - for 23 years. My masters' degree was in journalism at the University of Montana, and my thesis would be on the press during the Porfiriato. But I was also interested in the current problems of Mexico. A national election was coming up in a few days and had been the source of contention.

In one bar, a middle-aged Mexican asked me, "Do you smoke the marijuana?" Then he went on to explain that the federal government was moving into the drug trade, and since heroin and cocaine were much more profitable than the lowly weed, they had come into Northern Mexico and burned marijuana fields.

I continued to wander the streets, and just before midnight, I found myself in one of those hole-in-the-wall bars, where everything is back lit in soft red light, and the beer was a little more   expensive.
I fell into a conversation with a young man named Enrique, who had one of those memorable haircuts of the 1980s - his hair was long but stylish. We had a couple of beers, but I felt uncomfortable when he followed me into the restroom. What he was doing, I reasoned in hindsight, was checking out the secret pocket in which I kept my traveler's checks.

I decided it was time to leave. He followed me to the door, and as soon as I stepped outside, he and two other guys grabbed me and forced me into the backseat of a car. I was driven to the edge of town, and then transferred to a police car, where I sat between two rather large uniformed fellows. They drove out of town and then out a dirt road, where I was pulled out of the car. One of the large fellows hit me and I went down like a stone. I was not knocked out, but lay there as quietly as I could, since resistance would only mean more beating or worse. They reached down and got the travelers checks, and then they were gone.

After they drove away on the dirt road, I got up and walked the other way into the dark. I walked all night -- actually walked the soles off my boots. Just before dawn, I heard a dog barking and headed towards it. After a short time, I reached a small village. Some workers were getting into a pick-up truck to head to work across the border. I hitched a ride to a small border crossing about 20 miles east of El

Paso, and then hitch hiked back to town. When I told the American border guards what had happened, they just said, "good luck" getting any kind justice. My Congressman told me the same thing.

Two days later, I returned to Mexico, traveling by bus to Ciudad de Chihuahua, where I spent three days interviewing Margarita Terrazas, the daughter of Silvestre Terrazas. She was an older lady who greeted me with an *abrazo*. When I told her my story, she didn't think it was a simple robbery. I made the mistakes of identifying myself as a journalist and asking about drugs. A reporter from the El Paso paper made the same mistake, and he, too, got a one-way trip into the desert. He got back to El Paso, quit his job and moved back to New England.

I continued my journey on an express bus to Mexico City, where I stayed for three months. A week after I arrived, I walked down a street and saw a headline in the *Mexico City News*, the English-language newspaper. A reporter and her editor in Matamoros had been machined-gunned to death on the steps of their newspaper. The assailants got away through Brownsville, Texas. After that, I identified myself as a historian, not a journalist.

The man who brought me to Mexico was Filomeno Mata. For a graduate level, Mexican History course, I read *Precursors of the Mexican Revolution* by James Cockcroft. Mr. Cockcroft wrote about Señor Mata as a member of the opposition press during the Porfiriato, the reign of Porfirio Díaz. They were contemporaries and friendly acquaintances. Maybe not so friendly later: Mr. Cockcroft wrote that Mata went nine times to Belen - the prison where Don Porfirio housed errant journalists. My question was why Señor Mata kept doing what he was doing? As it turned out, Mr. Cockcroft got it wrong: Señor Mata did not go to Belen nine times. According to his son, he went more than 150 times, and after 1896, his jail visits became so common that Don Porfirio allowed him to keep his own bed in the prison.

I spent three months in Mexico from July to September 1986, and then returned the following January and came back in April. I spent my time reading old newspapers at UNAM and the National Archives, interviewing historians, journalism professors, and journalists. The research led to my thesis, "Porfirio Díaz and the Press: An Enduring Legacy of economic controls" and it was here I first learned about Ricardo Flores Magón. I was drawn to him as a writer. Otherwise, I pretty much accepted the standard historical view of the man: a revolutionary who became more left wing as time went on.

After graduate school, I went back to newspapering, and eventually drifted into teaching writing. I spent 20 years, as both a journalist and teacher, in American Indian Country. I taught writing in China for two years, and finally spent five years teaching at the American University of Nigeria. This changed me in several ways: I became aware of different cultures, and saw firsthand the impact of journalism on those societies. In Nigeria, newspapers are basically for sale. In China, you can certainly bribe your way into a feature story, but in both cases the media is massively controlled.

I was familiar with this sort of thing, because in Mexico, while I spent much of my time reading old Mexican newspapers, I also interviewed every journalist and journalism professor I could. The academics were much more forthcoming. When I crossed the border, one US Dollar bought 600 pesos (when I left for the last time, a U.S dollar brought 1100 pesos). An editor at a newspaper was paid 500 pesos a week.

But I also saw something else in Mexico I did not see in Nigeria or in Asia: I saw ordinary people running away from the police. One evening in late August 1986, I had a young uniformed officer approach me.

¿Usted es Norte Americano? (Are you an American?)

170

He led me to a fellow US citizen who had been badly beaten, and then staggered to a metro station in the Zona Rosa. It was a young man who had entered one too many dark streets. I asked the young officer if he had informed his superiors. He confided in me that it was probably his sergeant who had set the young man up. I helped get the young man off the street, and was a bit more careful in my own journeys.

I was forced into medical retirement in the end of 2014. I first moved back to Asia, and did not return to the United States until July 2015. While still in Asia, I became familiar with the work of Heribert von Feilitzsch, who has done the best research, at least in my mind, on the Mexican Revolution in recent years. We developed an e-mail dialogue, and spent three days in March 2016, talking almost non-stop. Several off-hand comments from these conversations renewed my interest in the role of Ricardo Flores Magón in the revolution, not as a precursor but literally as the man who started the fires that burned Mexico down. In my renewed research, I came to a different understanding of the man and his work. I came to appreciate his view of government, although I could never be in complete agreement with it. Flores Magón offered the intellectual and philosophical fuel of the revolution -- the other leaders basically were seeking rather limited reform, like Madero, or simply power, like Huerta, or their place in history, like Carranza, Obregon or Calles. Two charismatic leaders, Villa and Zapata, attracted the most fervent followers, but neither man wanted nor believed themselves capable enough to rule Mexico. The last truly revolutionary leader was President Lazaro Cardenas (1934-1940).

While working on this book, I came across the A&E produced documentary "Cartel land." In 2013, Matthew Heinman traveled to Mexico, and to the Arizona border area to record with his camera what was going on in that part of the world. The film opened with a scene of a man "cooking" methamphetamine in Mexico. "We come from poverty," the man says. "If we were doing well, we would be like you..." The film moves back and forth, telling the story of the rise of vigilante groups on both sides of the border. Things go badly for the leader of one of the vigilante groups on the Mexican side, and at the end of the film, Heinman returns to his original interview. The masked man is saying, "we are part of the government now, so we help everybody."

This book does not pretend to be a biography of Ricardo Flores Magón, but it is a story of journalism and betrayal. The Flores Magón brothers got into journalism, basically backing into the business through a legal journal. They found a hungry audience among the legal and journalism professions in Mexico. Ricardo and Enrique could build on that audience when they crossed the border in 1904, and they continued to build on that audience until both fled to Canada in 1906. The paper existed until 1907, when Ricardo went to prison the first time. He had long been an anarchist, but it was not something he learned simply from European authors. When he relaunched the PLM with himself as president, he lost support in Mexico and alienated a lot of people. When Madero won the initial round of the Mexican Revolution, Ricardo Flores Magón was radicalized too much – and by that time he was financially linked to the American – not the Mexican - left.

He felt betrayed by numerous associates who stayed true to the single purpose of the early revolution: to end the reign of Porfirio Díaz. Between 1910 and 1920, Mexicans butchered each other wholesale. At the end, they learned one thing, they learned how to run Mexico, and they learned it all from Porfirio Díaz.

After Madero, the men who ran Mexico - except for Lázaro Cárdenas - paid lip-service to the intellectual ideals pushed by the Flores Magón brothers from 1900 to 1906. After his death, the Mexican government gladly accepted Ricardo Flores Magón as a hero. The anarchists of the world took him on as their personal hero, and reproduced the writing he did after 1910. In large part, modern historians look at him through those lenses, and recount the botched revolts of 1906 and 1908, and the equally botched attempts at "revolution" on the Baja peninsula in 1910 and 1911.

When I was in Mexico, more than one savvy Mexican told me, "This country is ruled by six men, but nobody knows their names."

If one looks at the methods of how Don Porfirio ruled Mexico and looks at the PRI, and whatever name of the subsequent ruling parties, those methods are still very much in place.

American readers may think that this basically has nothing to do with them. When I was in Mexico in the 1980s, I did advertising surveys of ten major Mexico City dailies, and found that the more independent (or moving to the left) a paper was, the more likely it would have government subsidized advertising. I returned to the United States - this was in the days before the internet - and discovered that in the major dailies, corporations were the major buyers of newspaper advertisement. The Reagan Administration ended the Fair Doctrine Rule in broadcast journalism in 1986, giving rise to right wing talk radio. Rupert Murdoch changed his citizenship so he could launch Fox News, which sold US citizens on the idea that all media, other than Fox News, was biased toward the left.

What works in Mexico also works in the United States. We have become accustomed to new sacred cows. The majority of Americans want more gun control, but the National Rifle Association has made an extended second amendment right sacred. The majority of Americans want a single-payer health care system, but this has been continually shouted down and killed by lobbyists, and the medical industry is probably the greatest "sacred cow" of American journalism.

Regardless of what Ricardo Flores Magón believed or when he believed it, he started the brush fires that would eventually burn the old regime to the ground, simply by telling the truth.

Bibliography

Archival Materials

Díaz, Porfirio. Personal Archives, 1876-1916. Material from 1888. Universidad Iberoamericana. México.

Terrazas, Silvestre, Outgoing Correspondence and papers, 1893-1913. M-B. 18 Pt Box 83, Box 110-112. Bancroft Library. California University at Berkley.

Turner, Ethel Duffy. Assorted correspondence and published documents at Museo de Antropología, México.

US Department of State, Consular Dispatches from Mexico City. Record Group 59, National Archives, Washington, D.C.

Digital Archival Materials

Archivo Digital de Ricardo Flores Magón (http://archivomagon.net/periodicos/regeneracion-1900-1918/1ra-epoca), translations by the author.

Archivo Digital de Ricardo Flores Magón (http://archivomagon.net/periodicos/regeneracion-1900-1918/2da-epoca), translations by the author.

Interviews by Author

Beauregard, Mario. Freelance writer and broadcast commentator, former staff member of Ovaciónese, El Día and others. Interviewed in Mexico City, July 24 and March 11 and 16, 1987.

Dale-Lloyd, Jane. Instructor, Departamento de Historia, Universidad Iberoamericana. Oversees the cataloguing of the archives of Porfirio Díaz at UIA, and catalogued the archives of Ethel Duffy Turner at Museo de

Antropología. Interviewed in Mexico City, various dates, July, August, 1986, and March 11 and 16, 1987.

Molina, Gabriel. Jefe del Departamento de Comunicación, Universidad de las Américas. Interviewed in Puebla, March 9, 1987.

Molina, Ignacio. Instructor, Departamento de Historia, Universidad Iberoamericana. Interviewed in Mexico City, various dates, July and August, 1986. March 9, 1987, in Puebla.

Prieto, Francisco. Jefe del Departamento de Comunicación, Universidad Iberoamericana. Interviewed in Mexico City, March 23, 1987,

Septien, Jaimie. Instructor, Departamento de Comunicación, Universidad Iberoamericana and columnist for Uno Más Uno. Interviewed in Mexico City, March 23 and 25, 1987

Terrazas, Margarita, Daughter of Silvestre Terrazas. Interviewed in Chihuahua, Ch., Mexico, July 2, 3, and 4, 1986.

von Feilitzsch, Heribert. Independent researcher on Germany affairs during the Mexican Revolution. Interviewed in Albuquerque, New Mexico, USA, March 14 through 17, 2016.

Primary Source Material in other media

Heineman, Matthew. Producer. "Cartel Land" Documentary, 2015.

Feiser, Ruth, interview with Ethel Duffy Turner, 1966. Regional Oral History Office, Bancroft Library at UC Berkeley, available online at https://archive.org/details/cabeuroh_000119, retrieved June 9, 10, 2016.

Current News Reports

Marosi, Richard "Hardship on Mexico's farms, a bounty for US tables," December 7, 2014

Stevenson, Mark, "Mexico struggles to come to grip with treatment of Indians." Associated Press, February, 2001

Winfield, Nicole, Perez, Sonia, and Stevenson, Mark, "Pope Francis slams exploitation of Mexican Indians." Associated Press, February 15, 2016.

Magazines

The Border (various editions, 1909).

Colliers (various editions, 1900-1910).

Engineering and Mining Journal (1908).

Nation (various editions, 1900-1914).

New Republic (July 5, 1922).

Pearson's Magazine (March 1908).

Newspapers (during the Porfiriato)

Correo de Chihuahua (various editions, 1899-1913)

Diario del Hogar (various editions, 1881-1911) read hard copies of the paper at UNAM in Mexico City, in 1986-87

Great Falls Tribune (June, 1906; various editions 1910-1913)

El Paso Herald (1910).

El Paso Times (various editions, 1910-1914).

El Imparcial (editions published in January, 1900, 1905, 1906), various editions, 1900 to 1910).

New York Times (editions published in January, 1900, 1905, 1906, various editions 1886, 1904-1914).

El Pais (editions published in January, 1900, 1905, 1906, various editiong 1900-1910).

El Hijo de Ahuizote (various editions, 1892-1900 – Daniel Cabrera editor; 1892, Ricardo Flores Magón, editor).

Mexican Herald (editions published in January of 1900, 1905,1906, 1908; various editions 1900 to 1910).

New York Times (1900 to 1904, various editions, 1886; various editions, 1900 to 1900).

El País (editions published in January 1900, 1905, 1908; various editions, 1900 to 1910).

Regeneración (various editions, 1900 to 1918).

Primary Source Books

Altramirano, Graziella and Villa, Guadalupe, editors, *La Revolución Mexicana* (México: Secretaria de Educación Pública, 1985).

Cabrera, Luis. *La Revolución es la Revolución* (anthology of articles, 1908-1952) (Mexico, D.F. Partido Revolucionario Institucional Comisión Nacional del CEN, no publication date).

Creelman, James, *Díaz, Master of México* (New York: Appleton and Company, 1911).

Davis, Elmer. *The History of the New York Times, 1851-1921* (New York: New York Times Company, 1921).

Flores Magón, Ricardo, *Epistolario Revolucionario e Íntimo: 1921-1922,* edited by Práxedis, G. Güero (México: Ediciones Antorcha, 1975).

_____ *Epistolario y Textos de Ricardo Flores Magón*, edited by Manuel Gonzales Ramírez (México: Fondo de Cultura Económica, 1964).

______ *El Partido Liberal Mexicano, 1906-1908,* edited by Chantel López and Omar (Mexico: Ediciones Antorcha, 1986).

Furlong, Thomas, *Fifty Years a Detective* (St. Louis: C. E. Barnett, 1912).

De Fornaro, Carlo, *Díaz, Czar of Mexico* (New York: self-published, 1901).

Madero, Francisco, *La Sucesión Presidencial en 1910*, as reprinted in Meléndez, José T., *La Revolución Mexicana, Tomo II* (México: Unión Cooperativa de Artes Gráficas del D. F., 1940).

Mata, Luis, *Filomeno Mata: su vida y su labor* (México: Secretaria de Educación Pública, 1945).

Hanney, David, *Díaz* (New York: Henry Holt and Company, 1917).

Sierra, Justo, *The Political Evolution of the Mexican People,* translated by Charles Ramsdell (Austin and London: University of Texas Press, 1975).

Terrazas, Silvestre, *El Verdadero Pancho Villa* (Chihuahua: Talleres Gráficos de Gobierno del Estado de Chihuahua, 1984).

Turner, Ethel Duffy, *Ricardo Flores Magón y el Partido Liberal Mexicana* (Mexico: C.E.N. 1984).

________, *Revolution in Baja: Ricardo Flores Magon's High Noon* (Detroit: Blaine Ethridge Books, 1981).

Turner, John Kenneth, *Barbarous Mexico* (Austin: Austin University press, reprinted in 1975).

Verter, Mitchel Cowen, Bufe, Chaz, eds., *Dreams of Freedom: A Ricardo Flores Magón Reader* (Oakland: AK Press, 2006).

Seconday materials

Unpublished

Bravo, Esperanza Norma. "El Periodismo en la Revolución Mexicana." Tesis por Universidad Femenina de México, Escuela de Derecho y Ciencias Sociales, 1968.

Sandals, Robert Lynn, "Silvestre Terrazas, the Press and the Origins of the Mexican Revolution in Chihuahua," doctoral dissertation (Portland: Department of History, University of Oregon, 1967).

Uriaz Alveara, Patricia. "El Porfirismo a Través de sus Periódicos." Tesis por Departamento de Comunicación, Universidad Iberoamericana. 1976.

Books

Alameda, Francisco R. *La Emprenda y el periodismo en Chihuahua* (México: Gobierno del Estado de Chihuahua, 1943).

_____, Francisco R., *La Revolución en Estado de Chihuahua, Tomo I* (Chihuahua: Biblioteca del Instituto Nacional de Estudios Históricos de la Revolución Mexicana, 1964).

Albro, Ward S., *Always a Rebel: Ricardo Flores Magón and the Mexican Revolution* (Fort Worth: Texas Christian University Press, 1992).

Azuela, Mariano, translated by E. Munguía, Jr., *The Underdogs* (Original title, *Los De Abajo*) (New York: Signet, 1962).

Baker, Richard D, *Judicial Review in Mexico: A study of the Amparo Suit* (Austin: University of Texas Press, 1971).

Bazant, Milada, *Debate Pedagógico durante El Porfiriato* (México: Secretaria de Educación Pública, 1957).

Beals, Carleton, *Porfirio Díaz: Dictator of Mexico* (Philadelphia: JB Lippincott Company, 1932).

Beezley, William H. *Insurgent Governor: Abraham Gonzales and the Mexican Revolution in Chihuahua* (Lincoln: University of Nebraska Press, 1973).

Brading, D.A., *Caudillo and Peasant in the Mexican Revolution (*Cambridge: Cambridge University Press, 1977).

Brenner, Anita, Layton, George Ross, *The Wind that Swept Mexico* (Austin: University of Texas Press, 1971).

Buchenau, Jürgen, Gilbert, Joseph M., *Mexico's Once and Future Revolution: Social Upheaval and the Challenge of Rule Since the Late nineteenth Century (*Durham: Duke University Press, 2013).

Bufe, Chaz and Verter, Mitchell Cowen, eds., *Dreams of Freedom: a Ricardo Flores Magón Reader* (Canada: AK Press, 2006).

Bulnes, Francisco. *El Verdadero Díaz y la Revolución.* (México: Editora Nacional, 1952).

Calvert, Peter, *The Mexican Revolution, 1910-1914: The Diplomacy of Anglo-American Conflict* (Austin: University of Texas Press, 1968).

Cockcroft, James, *Intellectual Precursors of the Mexican Revolution, 1900-1913* (Boston: Cambridge University Press, 1968).

Cumberland, Charles Curtis, The *Mexican Revolution: Genesis under Madero* (New York: Greenwood Press, 1952).

Gage, Beverly, *The Day Wall Street exploded: A History of the American in its first Age of Terror* (New York, London: Oxford University Press, 2009).

Garcia, Mario T. *Desert Immigrants: The Mexicans of El Paso, 1880-1920* (New Haven Conn.: Yale University Press. 1981).

Godoy, Francisco, *Porfirio Díaz, Presidente de México, El Fundador de una Gran República* (Mexico: Muller, 1910).

Guzmán, Diego Arenas, *José María Pino Suarez* (Villahermosa: Gobierno del Estado de Tabasco, 1985).

_____, *Periodismo en la Revolución Mexicana*, (México: Biblioteca de Instituto Nacional de Estudios Históricos de La Revolución Mexicana, 1966).

Hanson, Roger D., *The Politics of Mexican Development* (Baltimore: John Hopkins University Press, 1984).

Harris, Charles H., Sadler, Louis R., *The Plan de San Diego: Tejano Rebellion, Mexican Intrigue* (Lincoln: University of Nebraska Press, 2013).

Hernando, Teodore, *Los Precursores de la Revolución* (México: Sin Editorial, 1944).

Hill, Larry D. *Emissaries to a Revolution, Woodrow Wilson's executive Agents in Mexico.* (Baton Rouge: Louisiana State University Press, 1973).

Kapp, Frank Averill, Jr., *The Life of Sebastian Lerdo de Tejada, 1823-1899: A study of Influence and Obscurity* (New York: Greenwood Press, 1968).

Katz, Friedrich and Lloyd, Jane Dale, *Porfirio Díaz frente al descontento Popular Regional, 1891-1893* (México: Universidad Iberoamericana, 1986).

_____*The Life and Times of Pancho Villa* (Stanford: Stanford University Press, 1998).

Kendall, Jonathan, *La Capital: A Biography of Mexico City* (New York: Henry Holt and Company, 1990).

Knight, Alan, *The Mexican Revolution, Volume 1: Porfirians, Liberals and Peasants* (Lincoln, London: University of Nebraska Press,1986).

Krauze, Enrique. *Porfirio Díaz, Místico de la Autoridad.* (México, D.F: Fondo de Cultura Económica, 1987).

Lister, Florence C. and Robert H. *Chihuahua, Storehouse of Storms.* (Albuquerque: University of New Mexico Press, 1965).

Lomnitz, Claudio, *The Return of the Comrade Ricardo Flores Magón* (New York: Zone Books, 2014).

Loret de Mola, Rafael. *Denuncia.* (México: Grijalbo, 1987).

Lloyd, Jane-Dale, *El Proceso de Modernización Capitalista en el Noroeste de Chihuahua* (Mexico: Universidad Iberoamericana, 1987).

Machado, Manuel, Jr., *The North Mexican Cattle Industry, 1910-1975: Ideology, Conflict, and Change* (College Station: Texas A&M University Press, 1981).

Magnor, James A., *Men of Mexico (*Freeport: Books for Libraries Press, 1942).

Mancisidor, José, *Historia de la Revolución Mexicana* (México: Costa-Amic Editores, no date).

Meyer, Michael C., *Mexican Rebel: Pascual Orozco and the Mexican Revolution.* (Lincoln: University of Nebraska Press, 1967).

_____ and Sherman, William L., *The Course of Mexican History* (Lincoln: University of Nebraska Press, 1967).

Poole, David, editor, *Land and Liberty: Anarchist influences in the Mexican Revolution – Ricardo Flores*

Magón, Second Edition (New York: Christie Books, 2012).

Quiñones, Amada Díaz, *Porfirio Díaz: Los Intelectuales y la Revolución* (México: El Callaíto, 1981).

Roeder, Ralph, *Hacia el México Moderno: Porfirio Díaz*, Volume II (México: Fonda de Cultura Económica, 1973).

Ross, Stanley R., editor, *Fuentes para la historia contemporánea de México: Periódicos y revistas* (México: El Colegio de México, 1965).

_____, *Francisco Madero: Apostle of the Mexican Revolution* (New York: Columbia University Press, 1955).

Santillán, Diego Abad de, *Ricardo Flores Magón: El Apóstol de la Revolución Social Mexicana* (México: Grupo Cultura, 1925).

Taracena, Alfonzo, *La Verdadera Revolución Mexicana*, (México: Editorial Jus, 1965).

Trowbridge, Edward D. *Mexico To-Day and To-Morrow* (New York: Macmillan Company, 1911).

Ugarte, José Bravo, *Periodistas y Periódicos Mexicanos* (México: México Heroico Editorial, 1966).

Wasserman, Mark, *Capitalist, Caciques, and Revolution: The Native Elite and Foreign Enterprise in Chihuahua, Mexico, 1854- 1911* (Chapel Hill: University of North Carolina Press, 1984).

Wolf, Eric R., *Peasant Wars of the 20th Century* (New York: Harper books, 1969).

Valadez, José C., *El Porfirismo: Historia de un Régimen* (México, DF: Editorial Patriar, 1946).

Von Feilitzsch, Heribert, *In Plain Sight: Felix A. Sommerfeld, Spymaster in Mexico, 1908-1914* (Amissville: Henselstone Verlag, 2012).

_____, *Felix A. Sommerfeld and the Mexican Front in the Great War* (Amissville: Henselstone Verlag, 2015).

_____, *The Secret War Council: The German Fight against the Entente in 1914* (Amissville: Henselstone Verlag, 2015).

_____, *The Secret War on the United States in 1915: A Tale of Sabotage, Labor Unrest and Border Troubles* (Amissville: Henselstone Verlag, 2015).

Zea, Leopoldo, *Positivism in Mexico*, translated by Josephine H. Schule (Austin: University of Texas Press, 1974).

Articles

Cockcroft, James D. "El Maestro de Primaria en la Revolución Mexicana." *Historia Moderna de México*, Vol. VIII, April – June, 1967, pp. 567-584.

De María y Campos, Alfonso, "Porfirianos Prominentes: Origines y Anos de Juventud de Ocho Integrantes del Grupo de los Científicos, 1846-1876" (*Historia Mexicana*, Volume XXXIV, 4, April-June, 1985).

Gonzales, Gaspar Estrada, "Mexico As It Is," *Sunset Magazine,* Volume 24, January-June, 1910.

Owen, Roger C. "Indians and Revolution: The 1911 Invasion of Baja," *California" Ethnohistory* 10, no. 4, pp. 373-395.

Turner, Frederick, "Anti-Americanism in Mexico, 1910-1913" *Hispanic Historical Review.* Volume XLVII, November, 1967. pp. 501-518.

Wood, Andrew Grant, "Death of a political Prisoner: Revisiting the case of Ricardo Flores Magón *(A Contracorriente Magazine*, University of Tulsa, no date), accessed at https://www.ncsu.edu/project/acontracorriente/fall_05/Wood.pdf. Retrieved July 20, 2016.

Index